Rick Steves'

SNAPSHOT

Madrid & Toledo

P9-DTC-607

CONTENTS

INTRODUCTION

This Snapshot guide, excerpted from my guidebook *Rick Steves' Spain 2010*, introduces you to majestic Madrid. Spain's capital is home to some of Europe's top art treasures (the Prado Museum's collection, plus Picasso's *Guernica* in the Reina Sofía) and a lively selection of characteristic tapas bars, where you can assemble a memorable feast of Spanish specialties. Explore the city's cozy-feeling historic core, tour its lavish Royal Palace, and beat the heat on a rowboat at the lush and inviting Retiro Park.

This book also covers several side-trips from Madrid. Toledo, the hill-capping onetime capital of Spain, features one of the country's most magnificent cathedrals, a medieval vibe, and top paintings by favorite son El Greco. Northwest of Madrid, you'll find Spain's grandest palace at the Inquisition-era El Escorial, a jarring jolt of the 20th century at Franco's Valley of the Fallen, and a pair of charming towns: Segovia, with its towering Roman aqueduct, and Ávila, encircled by a medieval wall.

To help you have the best trip possible, I've included the following topics in this book:

• **Planning Your Time,** with advice on how to make the most of your limited time

• **Orientation,** including tourist information (abbreviated as TI), tips on public transportation, local tour options, and helpful hints

• **Sights** with ratings:

▲▲▲—Don't miss

▲▲—Try hard to see

▲—Worthwhile if you can make it

No rating Worth knowing about

• **Sleeping** and **Eating,** with good-value recommendations in every price range

• **Connections,** with tips on trains, buses, and driving

Practicalities, near the end of this book, has information on money, phoning, hotel reservations, transportation, and other helpful hints, plus Spanish survival phrases.

To travel smartly, read this little book in its entirety before you go. It's my hope that this guide will make your trip more meaning-ful and rewarding. Traveling like a temporary local, you'll get the absolute most out of every mile, minute, and euro.

Buen viaje!

MADRID

Today's Madrid is upbeat and vibrant, still enjoying a post-Franco renaissance. You'll feel it. Even the living-statue street performers have a twinkle in their eyes.

Madrid is the hub of Spain. This modern capital—Europe's highest, at more than 2,000 feet—has a population of 3.2 million. Like its people, the city is relatively young. In 1561, when Spain ruled the world's most powerful empire, King Philip II decided to move his capital from Toledo to Madrid. One hundred years ago, Madrid had only 400,000 people—so the majority of today's Madrid is modern sprawl surrounding an intact, easy-to-navigate historic core.

To support their bid to host the 2012 Olympics, Madrid began some massive city-improvement building projects. Although they lost, the construction continues as if they won. Politicians who back these projects have been rewarded both financially (locals claim some corrupt officials are getting kickbacks) and politically—residents love to see all the new squares, pedestrian streets, beltway tunnels, parks, and Metro stations popping up. As the city eyes another Olympics bid for 2016, construction won't let up soon.

Madrid's ambitious improvement plans include the creation of a wonderful new pedestrian street crossing the city from the Prado to the Royal Palace. Strolling Calle de las Huertas from Plaza Mayor to the Prado (and the newly pedestrianized Calle del Arenal), you see how the investment is turning ramshackle zones into trendy ones. A new macro-Metro station near Puerta del Sol—to accommodate a new, super-efficient commuter line connecting the two train stations and the main square—is due to be finished in 2010.

MADRID

By installing posts to keep cars off sidewalks, making the streets safer after dark, and restoring old buildings, Madrid is working hard to make itself more livable...and fun to visit.

Tourists are the real winners. Dive headlong into the grandeur and intimate charm of Madrid. The lavish Royal Palace, with its gilded rooms and frescoed ceilings, rivals Versailles. The Prado has Europe's top collection of paintings. The city's huge Retiro Park invites you to take a shady siesta and hopscotch through a mosaic of lovers, families, skateboarders, pets walking their masters, and expert bench-sitters. Save time for Madrid's elegant shops and people-friendly pedestrian zones. On Sundays, cheer for the bull at a bullfight or bargain like mad at a mega-size flea market. Lively Madrid has enough street-singing, bar-hopping, and people-watching vitality to give any visitor a boost of youth.

Planning Your Time

Divide your time between Madrid's top three attractions: the Royal Palace (worth a half-day), the Prado Museum (also worth a half-day), and its bar-hopping contemporary scene. On a Sunday, consider allotting extra time for the flea market (year-round) and/or a bullfight (some Sundays Easter–mid-Oct, especially during San Isidro festival mid-May).

Madrid is worth two days and three nights on even the fastest trip. I'd spend them this way:

Day 1: Take a brisk 20-minute good-morning-Madrid walk from Puerta del Sol to the Prado (from Puerta del Sol, walk three blocks south to Plaza del Ángel, then take the pedestrianized Calle de las Huertas). Spend the rest of the morning at the Prado, then take an afternoon siesta in Retiro Park, or tackle modern art at the Centro de Arte Reina Sofía (Picasso's *Guernica*) and/or the Thyssen-Bornemisza Museum. Ride bus #27 from the Prado out through Madrid's modern section for a dose of the non-touristy, no-nonsense big city. Have dinner at 20:00, with tapas around Plaza Santa Ana.

Day 2: Follow my "Welcome to Madrid" self-guided walk, tour the Royal Palace, and have lunch at Café Oriente or near Plaza Mayor. Your afternoon is free for other sights, shopping, or a side-trip to El Escorial (closed Mon; see next chapter). Be out at the magic hour—before sunset—when beautifully lit people fill Madrid.

Note that many top sights are closed on Monday, including the Prado, Thyssen-Bornemisza Museum, and El Escorial; sights remaining open on Monday include the Royal Palace (open daily) and Centro de Arte Reina Sofía (closed Tue). For good day-trip possibilities from Madrid, see the next two chapters (Northwest of Madrid and Toledo).

Madrid

MADRID

Orientation to Madrid

Puerta del Sol marks the center of Madrid. No major sight is more than a 20-minute walk or a €4 taxi ride from this central square. The Royal Palace (to the west) and the Prado Museum and Retiro Park (to the east) frame Madrid's historic center. This zone can be covered on foot. Southwest of Puerta del Sol is a 17th-century district with the slow-down-and-smell-the-cobbles Plaza Mayor and memories of preindustrial Spain. North of Puerta del Sol runs Calle de Gran Vía, and between the two are lively pedestrian shopping streets. Gran Vía, bubbling with shops and cinemas, leads to the modern Plaza de España. From the Prado, the Paseo de la Castellana is a straight boulevard cutting north through the modern town to the "gateway to Europe" towers. Between Puerta del Sol and the Atocha train station stretches the colorful, up-and-coming multiethnic Lavapiés district (see the "The Lavapiés District Tapas Crawl").

Tourist Information

Madrid's many TIs share a phone number (tel. 915-881-636) and website (www.esmadrid.com).

The best TI is on **Plaza Mayor** (daily 9:30–20:30, air-con, limited free Internet access). It's centrally located and innovative, offering several €4 English guided walks a day (described later in "Tours in Madrid") and a free downloadable MP3 self-guided tour. They also provide the SATE police service to aid foreigners who've run into trouble.

Madrid's other TIs have the same hours (Mon–Sat 8:00–20:00, Sun 9:00–14:00): near the **Prado Museum** (Duque de Medinaceli 2, behind Palace Hotel); **Chamartín train station** (near track 20); **Atocha train station** (in AVE side); and **airport** (Terminal 1 and Terminal 4). Small info kiosks are in **Plaza de Callao** and in **Plaza de Cibeles** (daily 9:30–20:00).

At any TI, pick up a map, the handy *Traveler's Tips* booklet, the *Es Madrid* English-language monthly, and confirm your sightseeing plans. The TI's free *Public Transport* map is very well-designed to meet travelers' needs and has the most detailed map of the center. Get this and use it. TIs have the latest on bullfights and *zarzuela* (light Spanish opera). Only the most hyperactive travelers could save money buying the **Madrid Card,** which covers 40 museums and the Madrid Vision bus tour (€45/24 hrs, €58/48 hrs, €72/72 hrs).

For entertainment listings, the TI's printed material is not very good. Pick up the Spanish-language weekly entertainment guide ***Guía del Ocio*** (€1, sold at newsstands) or check their complete website: www.guiadelocio.com. It lists daily live music *("Conciertos"),* museums *("Museos"*—with the latest times and special exhibits), restaurants (an exhaustive listing), kids' activities *("Los Niños"),* TV schedules, and movies (*"V.O."* means original version, "*V.O. en inglés sub*" means a movie is played in English with Spanish subtitles rather than dubbed).

If you're heading to other destinations in Spain, stop by the Plaza Mayor office, which often has free maps and brochures (in English). Since many small-town TIs keep erratic hours and run out of these pamphlets, get what you can in Madrid. You can also get schedules for buses and some trains, allowing you to avoid unnecessary trips to the various stations. The TI's free and amazingly informative *Mapa de Comunicaciones España* is a road map of Spain that lists all the tourist offices and highway SOS numbers. (If they're out, ask for the route map sponsored by the Paradores hotel chain, the camping map, or the golf map.)

For tips on sightseeing, hotels, and more, visit www.madridman.com, run with passion by American Scott Martin.

Arrival in Madrid
By Train
Madrid's two train stations, Chamartín and Atocha, are both on Metro lines with easy access to downtown Madrid. (For Atocha Station, use the "Atocha RENFE" Metro stop; the stop named simply "Atocha" is farther from the station.) Chamartín handles most international trains and the AVE train to Segovia. Atocha generally covers southern Spain, as well as the AVE trains to Barcelona, Córdoba, Sevilla, and Toledo. Both stations offer long-distance trains *(largo recorrido)* as well as smaller local trains *(regionales* and *cercanías)* to nearby destinations.

Buying Tickets: You can buy tickets at the stations, at a travel agency, or online. Convenient travel agencies for buying tickets in Madrid include the El Corte Inglés Travel Agency at Atocha (Mon–Fri 7:00–22:00, Sat–Sun only for urgent arrangements, on ground floor of AVE side at the far end) and the El Corte Inglés department store at Puerta del Sol (see "Helpful Hints").

Traveling Between Chamartín and Atocha Stations: To travel between the two stations, you can take the Metro (line 1, 30–40 min, €1, see "Getting Around Madrid"), but the *cercanías* trains are faster (6/hr, 12 min, €1.15, free with railpass or any train ticket to Madrid—show it at ticket window in the middle of the turnstiles, departs from Atocha's track 2 and generally Chamartín's track 1, 3, 8, or 9—but check the *Salidas Inmediatas* board to be sure). A faster Atocha–Sol–Chamartín *cercanías* line is supposed to be completed in 2010.

Chamartín Station
The TI is opposite track 19. The impressively large information, tickets, and customer-service office is at track 11. You can relax in the Sala VIP Club if you have a first-class railpass and first-class seat or sleeper reservations (between tracks 13 and 14, cooler of free drinks). Luggage storage *(consignas)* is across the street, opposite track 17. The station's Metro stop is also called Chamartín (not "Pinar de Chamartín").

Atocha Station
The station is split in two: an AVE side (mostly long-distance trains) and a *cercanías* side (mostly local trains to the suburbs or *cercanías* and the Metro for connecting into downtown). These two parts are connected by a corridor of shops. Each side of the station has separate schedules and customer-service offices. The TI, which is in the AVE side, offers tourist info, but no train info (Mon–Sat 9:00–20:00, Sun 9:00–14:00, tel. 915-284-630).

There are three ticket offices at Atocha: The *cercanías* side has a small office for local trains and a big office for major trains (such as

MADRID

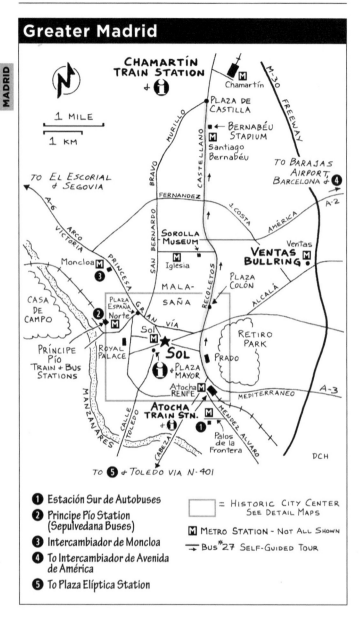

Greater Madrid

CHAMARTÍN
TRAIN STATION

Chamartín

PLAZA DE
CASTILLA

M-30 FREEWAY

BERNABÉU
STADIUM
Santiago
Bernabéu

TO BARAJAS
AIRPORT,
BARCELONA & ❹

1 MILE

1 KM

MURILLO

CASTELLANO

TO EL ESCORIAL
& SEGOVIA

A-6

ARCO VICTORIA

BRAVO

SAN BERNARDO

FERNANDEZ

J. COSTA

AMÉRICA

A-2

SOROLLA
MUSEUM

Ventas

VENTAS
BULLRING

Moncloa M

❸

PRINCESA

SAN

Iglesia

RECOLETOS

PLAZA
COLÓN

ALCALÁ

CASA
DE
CAMPO

PLAZA
ESPAÑA

❷ Norte
M

MALA-
SAÑA

GRAN

VÍA

Sol
M

RETIRO
PARK

PRÍNCIPE
PÍO
TRAIN & BUS
STATIONS

ROYAL
PALACE

★ SOL

PLAZA
MAYOR

PRADO

MANZANARES

CALLE
TOLEDO

Atocha
RENFE

ATOCHA
TRAIN STN.

MÉNDEZ ALVARO

MEDITERRANEO

A-3

M

CABEZA

Palos
de la
Frontera

❶

DCH

TO ❺ & TOLEDO VIA N-401

❶ Estación Sur de Autobuses
❷ Príncipe Pío Station
    (Sepulvedana Buses)
❸ Intercambiador de Moncloa
❹ To Intercambiador de Avenida
    de América
❺ To Plaza Elíptica Station

☐ = HISTORIC CITY CENTER
      SEE DETAIL MAPS

M METRO STATION - NOT ALL SHOWN
⇀ BUS #27 SELF-GUIDED TOUR

AVE). The AVE side has a pleasant, airy ticket office that also sells tickets for AVE and other long-distance trains (there are two lines: "Advance Sale" or "Selling Out Today"). If the line at one office is long, check the other offices. Grab a number from a machine to get your turn in line. For major destinations (such as Barcelona, San Sebastián, or Córdoba), you can use your credit card to avoid the lines—look for the ATM-like touch-screen machines to the right of the entrance.

Atocha's **AVE side,** which is in the towering old-station building, is remarkable for the lush, tropical garden filling its grand hall. It has the slick AVE trains, other fast trains (Grandes Líneas), a pharmacy (daily 8:00–22:00, facing garden), and the wicker-elegant Samarkanda— both an affordable cafeteria (daily 13:00–20:00) and a pricey restaurant (daily from 21:00, tel. 915-309-746). Luggage storage *(consigna)* is below Samarkanda (daily 6:00–22:20). In the departure lounge on the upper floor, TV monitors announce track numbers. For information, try the *Información* counter (daily 6:30–22:30), next to Centro Servicios AVE (which handles only AVE changes and problems). The *Atención al Cliente* office deals with problems on Grandes Líneas (daily 6:30–23:30). Also on the AVE side is the Club AVE/Sala VIP, a lounge reserved solely for AVE business-class travelers and for first-class ticket-holders or Eurailers with a first-class reservation (upstairs, past the security check on right; free drinks, newspapers, showers, and info service).

On the *cercanías* **side** of Atocha Station, you'll find the local *cercanías* trains, *regionales* trains, some eastbound faster trains, and the "Atocha RENFE" Metro stop. The *Atención al Cliente* office in the *cercanías* section has information only on trains to destinations near Madrid.

Terrorism Memorial: The terrorist bombings of March 11, 2004, took place in Atocha and on local lines going into and out of the station. Security is understandably tight here. A moving memorial is in the *cercanías* part of the station near the Atocha RENFE Metro stop. Walk inside and under the cylinder to read the thousands of condolence messages in many languages (daily 10:00–20:00). Its 36-foot cylindrical glass memorial towers are visible from outside on the street.

MADRID

By Bus

Madrid has several bus stations: Príncipe Pío (for Segovia, Metro: Príncipe Pío); Estación Sur Autobuses (for Ávila and Granada, Metro: Méndez Álvaro); Plaza Elíptica (for Toledo, Metro: Plaza Elíptica); Estación Intercambiador (for El Escorial, Metro: Moncloa); and Intercambiador de Avenida de América (for Pamplona and Burgos, Metro: Avenida de América). For details, see "Connections" at the end of this chapter.

By Plane

For information on Madrid's Barajas Airport, see the end of this chapter.

Helpful Hints

Theft Alert: Be wary of pickpockets, anywhere, anytime. Areas of particular risk are Puerta del Sol (the central square), El Rastro (the flea market), Gran Vía (the paseo zone: Plaza del Callao to Plaza de España), the Ópera Metro station (or anywhere on the Metro), bus #27, the airport, and any crowded streets. Be alert to the people around you: Someone wearing a heavy jacket in the summer is likely a pickpocket. Lately, Romanian teenagers dress like American teens and work the areas around the three big art museums; being under 18, they can't be arrested by the police. Assume a fight or any commotion is a scam to distract people about to become victims of a pickpocket. Wear your money belt. The small streets north of Gran Vía are particularly dangerous, even before nightfall. Muggings occur, but are rare. For help, see the next listing.

Tourist Emergency Aid: SATE is a centrally located police office offering emergency aid to victims of theft. Help ranges from canceling stolen credit cards to assistance in reporting a crime (daily 9:00–22:00, near Plaza de Santo Domingo at Calle Leganitos 19, 24-hr tel. 902-102-112, English spoken once you get connected to a person). The Plaza Mayor TI is a kind of SATE branch.

Prostitution: Diverse by European standards, Madrid is spilling over with immigrants from South America, North Africa, and Eastern Europe. Many young women come here, fall on hard times, and end up on the streets. While it's illegal to make money from someone else selling sex (i.e., pimping), prostitutes over 18 can solicit legally (€30, FYI). Calle de la Montera (leading from Puerta del Sol to Plaza Red de San Luis) is lined with what looks like a bunch of high-school girls skipping out of school for a cigarette break. Again, don't stray north of Gran Vía around Calle de la Luna and

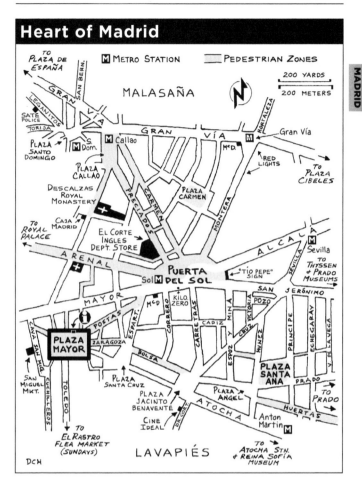

Heart of Madrid

- **M** METRO STATION
- PEDESTRIAN ZONES

TO PLAZA DE ESPAÑA

SAN BERN.

GRAN

LEGANITOS

MALASAÑA

200 YARDS

200 METERS

N

SATE POLICE

TORIJA

PLAZA SANTO DOMINGO

S. Dom. **M** **M** Callao

GRAN VÍA **M** Gran Vía

HORTALEZA

M^cD.

RED LIGHTS

TO PLAZA CIBELES

PLAZA CALLAO

DESCALZAS ROYAL MONASTERY

PRECIADOS

CARMEN

PLAZA CARMEN

MONTERA

CAJA MADRID

TO ROYAL PALACE

EL CORTE INGLES DEPT. STORE

A R E N A L

ALCALA

SEVILLA

M Sevilla

TO THYSSEN & PRADO MUSEUMS

PUERTA
Sol **M** **DEL SOL**

"TIO PEPE" SIGN

SAN JERÓNIMO

M A Y O R

POZO

M^cD

KILO ZERO

CARRERAS

CADIZ

MINA

VICTORIA

CRUZ

NUÑEZ

PRINCIPE

ECHEGARAY

V. DE LA VEGA

POSTAS

ESPARTE

CORREO

ESPOZ Y

PLAZA MAYOR

ZARAGOZA

CAVA SAN MIG

BOLSA

PLAZA SANTA ANA

PRADO

SAN MIGUEL MKT.

TOLEDO

CUCHILLEROS

PLAZA SANTA CRUZ

PLAZA JACINTO BENAVENTE

PLAZA ANGEL

A T O C H A

DATOR

HUERTAS

TO PRADO

CINE IDEAL

Anton Martin **M**

TO EL RASTRO FLEA MARKET (SUNDAYS)

LAVAPIÉS

TO ATOCHA STN. & REINA SOFIA MUSEUM

DCH

Plaza Santa María Soledad—while the streets may look inviting...this area is a meat-eating flower.

Embassies: The US Embassy is at Serrano 75 (tel. 915-872-200); the Canadian Embassy is at Nuñez de Balboa 35 (tel. 914-233-250).

One-Stop Shopping: The dominant department store is **El Corte Inglés,** which takes up several huge buildings in the commercial pedestrian zone just off Puerta del Sol (Mon–Sat 10:00–22:00, Sun 11:00–21:00, navigate with the help of the info desk near the door of the main building—the tallest building with the biggest sign, Preciados 3, tel. 913-798-000). They give out fine, free Madrid maps. In the main building, you'll find two handy travel agencies (see listing at end of this

MADRID

section), a post office, a modern cafeteria (seventh floor), and a supermarket with a fancy "Club del Gourmet" section in the basement. Across the street is its Librería branch—a huge bookstore. The second building fronting Puerta del Sol contains six floors of music, computers, home electronics, and SIM cards for mobile phones, with a box office on the top floor selling tickets to whatever's on in town. Locals figure you'll find anything you need at El Corte Inglés. Salespeople wear flag pins indicating which languages they can speak.

Internet Access: There are plenty of centrally located places to check your email. Any *locutorio* call center should have a few computers and is generally the cheapest. Near Plaza Santa Ana (and great if you're waiting for the tapas-crawl action to heat up), **La Bolsa de Minutos** has plenty of fast terminals (daily 9:30–24:00, Calle Espoz y Mina 17, tel. 915-322-622). **BBIG** has more than 100 terminals, is non-smoking, and seats casual Internet surfers apart from noisy, intense gamers (daily 9:30–24:00, at the corner of Puerta del Sol and the street that connects it to Plaza Mayor, at Mayor 1—on the second floor above Sol Park casino, tel. 915-312-364). Both places have disc-burning services and a helpful staff.

Phone Cards: You can buy cheap international phone cards at some newsstands, at Internet cafés, or at the easy-to-find *locutorio* call centers (but these are generally uncomfortable places to sit and talk). When choosing a phone card, remember that toll-free numbers start with 900, whereas 901 and 902 numbers can be expensive. Ask your hotel if they charge for the 900 number before making calls.

Bookstores: For books in English, try **FNAC Callao** (Calle Preciados 28, tel. 915-956-100), **Casa del Libro** (English on ground floor in back, Gran Vía 29, tel. 915-212-219), and **El Corte Inglés** (guidebooks and some fiction, in its Librería branch kitty-corner from main store, fronting Puerta del Sol—see "One-Stop Shopping," on previous page).

Laundry: Onda Blu will wash, dry, and fold your laundry (€5 self-service, €8 full-service, daily 9:30–22:00, León 3, east of Plaza Santa Ana, tel. 913-695-071, Ana). **Express Laundry Service** is a tiny shop that offers full-service laundry (€7 to wash and dry a big load, generally same-day service, Mon–Sat 9:30–20:30, closed Sun, between Puerto del Sol and Plaza Santa Ana at Calle Espoz y Mina 22, mobile 679-060-239).

Travel Agencies: The grand department store **El Corte Inglés** has two travel agencies (air and rail tickets, but not reservations for railpass-holders, €2 fee, on first and seventh floors, Mon–Sat 10:00–22:00, Sun 11:00–21:00, just off Puerta del Sol, tel. 913-798-000).

MADRID

Madrid Metro

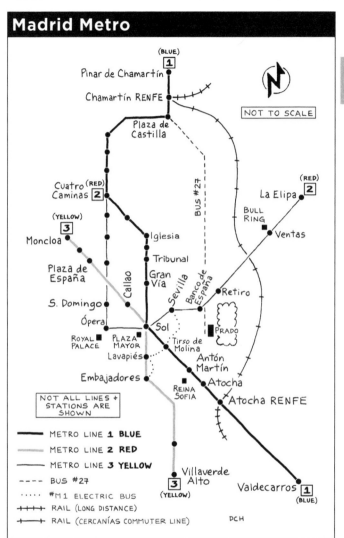

Pinar de Chamartín (BLUE) **1**
Chamartín RENFE
Plaza de Castilla
NOT TO SCALE
Cuatro Caminas (RED) **2**
La Elipa (RED) **2**
BUS #27
BULL RING
Ventas
Moncloa (YELLOW) **3**
Iglesia
Plaza de España
Tribunal
Gran Vía
Callao
Sevilla
Banco de España
Retiro
S. Domingo
Ópera
Sol
PRADO
ROYAL PALACE
PLAZA MAYOR
Tirso de Molina
Lavapiés
Antón Martín
Embajadores
REINA SOFIA
Atocha
Atocha RENFE

NOT ALL LINES + STATIONS ARE SHOWN

—— METRO LINE **1** BLUE
—— METRO LINE **2** RED
—— METRO LINE **3** YELLOW
---- BUS #27
····· #M1 ELECTRIC BUS
++++ RAIL (LONG DISTANCE)
+—+ RAIL (CERCANÍAS COMMUTER LINE)

Villaverde Alto
3 (YELLOW)
Valdecarros **1** (BLUE)

DCH

Getting Around Madrid

If you want to use Madrid's excellent public transit, my two best tips are these: Pick up and study the fine *Public Transit* map/flier (available at TIs), and take full advantage of the cheap 10-ride Metrobus ticket deal (see below).

By Metro: The city's broad streets can be hot and exhausting. A subway trip of even a stop or two saves time and energy. Madrid's Metro is simple, speedy, and cheap (€1/ride within zone A—which covers most of the city, but not trains out to the airport;

runs 6:00–1:30 in the morning, www.metromadrid.es or www
.ctm-madrid.es). The 10-ride Metrobus ticket can be shared by several travelers and works on both the Metro and buses (€7.40—or
€0.74 per ride, sold at kiosks, tobacco shops, and in Metro). Insert
your Metrobus ticket in the turnstile (it usually shows how many
rides remain on it), then retrieve it as you pass through. Stations
offer free system maps (see basic map of three main lines on previous page). Navigate by Metro stops (shown on city maps). To
transfer, follow signs to the next Metro line (numbered and color-
coded). The names of the end stops are used to indicate directions.
Green *salida* signs point to the exit. Using neighborhood maps and
street signs to exit smartly saves lots of walking. And watch out for
thieves.

By Bus: City buses, while not as easy as the Metro, can be
useful (€1 tickets sold on bus, or €7.40 for a 10-ride Metrobus
ticket—see above; bus maps at TI or info booth on Puerta del
Sol, poster-size maps are usually posted at bus stops, buses run
6:00–24:00, much less frequent *Buho* buses run all night).

By Taxi: Madrid's 15,000 taxis are reasonably priced and easy
to hail. Foursomes travel as cheaply by taxi as by Metro. A ride
from the Royal Palace to the Prado costs about €4. After the €2
drop charge, the per-kilometer rate depends on the time: *Tarifa
1* (€1/kilometer) should be charged Mon–Sat 6:00–22:00; *Tarifa
2* (€1.10/kilometer) is valid after 22:00 and on Sundays and holidays. If your cabbie uses anything rather than *Tarifa 1* on weekdays
(shown as an isolated "1" on the meter), you're being cheated. Rates
can be higher if you go outside Madrid. Other legitimate charges
include the €5.50 supplement for the airport, the €3 supplement for
train or bus stations, and €13.50 per hour for waiting. Make sure
the meter is turned on as soon as you get into the cab so the driver
can't tack anything onto the official rate. If the driver starts adding
up "extras," look for the sticker detailing all legitimate surcharges
(which should be on the passenger window).

Tours in Madrid

Discover Madrid—The Plaza Mayor TI organizes a daily schedule of cheap, interesting guided walks. Tours last about 90 minutes,
are in English only, cost €4, and depart daily—generally from the
Plaza Mayor TI at 10:00, 12:00, and 16:00. Groups are often very
small, so you almost feel like you have a private guide. Just buy
your ticket at the TI a few minutes before departure.

Madrid Vision Hop-On, Hop-Off Bus Tours—Madrid Vision
offers two different hop-on, hop-off circuits of the city: historic
and modern. Buy a ticket from the driver (€17/1 day, €21/2 days)
and you can hop from sight to sight and route to route as you like,

listening to a recorded English commentary along the way. Each route has about 15 stops and takes about 90 minutes, with buses departing every 10 or 20 minutes. The two routes intersect at the south side of Puerta del Sol and in front of Starbucks across from the Prado (daily 9:30–24:00 in summer, 10:00–19:00 in winter, tel. 917-791-888, www.madridvision.es).

LeTango Tours—Carlos Galvin, a Spaniard who speaks flawless English (and has led tours for my groups since 1998), and his wife from Seattle, Jennifer, offer private tours in Madrid and other parts of Spain. Carlos mixes a market walk in the historic center with a culinary-and-tapas crawl to get close to the Madrileños, their culture, and their food. His walk gives a fine three-hour orientation and introduction to the fascinating and tasty culture of Madrid, plus travel tips (€95 per person, 10 percent cash discount, includes tastes in the market and light tapas at the end, minimum 2 people, alcohol-free and gourmet versions available, family-friendly, price goes down with more people). They also offer city, regional, and all-Spain tours and Madrid apartment rentals (about €170/night for 4 people) as explained on their website (tel. 913-694-752, mobile 661-752-458, www.letango.com, info@letango.com).

Local Guides—**Frederico and Cristina** are licensed guides who lead city walks through the pedestrian streets of the historic core of Madrid. Fred, Cris, and their team offer an all-ages tour of the big museums, including the Royal Palace, the Prado, and the Reina Sofía, as well as a tapas tour. Or, if you're looking to get outside Madrid, consider their guided tour to surrounding towns using public transit (per-tour costs: Mon–Fri €160, Sat–Sun €190, 10 percent Rick Steves discount, admissions and tapas not included, 3–5 hours, tel. 913-102-974, mobile 649-936-222, www.spainfred .com, spainfred@gmail.com).

Inés Muñiz Martin is a good guide for Madrid and the region (€140 for up to 4 hours, €170 on weekends and holidays, these rates include discount for Rick Steves readers, mobile 629-147-370, www.immguidedtours.com, info@immguidedtours.com).

Susana Jarabo, with a master's in art history, is another excellent independent guide (mobile 667-027-722, susanjarabo@yahoo .com).

Hernán Amaya Satt directs a group of licensed guides who take individuals around Madrid by foot or by car on 18 personalized tours (rates vary according to tour and number of people, 20 percent discount off official rates for Rick Steves readers, mobile 680-450-231, www.madrid-museum-tours.org, info@madrid -museum-tours.org).

Stephen Drake-Jones, a British expat, gives walks of historic old Madrid almost daily. A historian with a passion for the Duke

MADRID

Madrid at a Glance

▲▲▲**Prado Museum** One of the world's great museums, loaded with masterpieces by Diego Velázquez, Francisco de Goya, El Greco, Hieronymus Bosch, Albrecht Dürer, and more. **Hours:** Tue–Sun 9:00–20:00, closed Mon. See page 30.

▲▲▲**Royal Palace** Spain's sumptuous, lavishly furnished national palace. **Hours:** April–Sept Mon–Sat 9:00–19:00, Sun 9:00–16:00; Oct–March Mon–Sat 9:30–18:00, Sun 9:00–15:00. See page 24.

▲▲▲**Centro de Arte Reina Sofía** Modern-art museum featuring Picasso's epic masterpiece *Guernica*. **Hours:** Mon and Wed–Sat 10:00–21:00, Sun 10:00–14:30, closed Tue. See page 43.

▲▲**Puerta del Sol** Madrid's lively central square. **Hours:** Always bustling. See page 16.

▲▲**Thyssen-Bornemisza Museum** A great complement to the Prado, with lesser-known yet still impressive works and an especially good Impressionist collection. **Hours:** Tue–Sun 10:00–19:00, closed Mon. See page 42.

▲▲**Bullfight** Spain's controversial pastime. **Hours:** Scattered Sundays and holidays March–mid-Oct, plus almost daily May–early June. See page 51.

▲**Zarzuela** Madrid's delightful light opera. **Hours:** Evenings. See page 53.

▲**Plaza Mayor** Historic cobbled square. **Hours:** Always open. See page 20.

▲**Retiro Park** Festive green escape from the city, with rental rowboats and great people-watching. **Hours:** Closes at dusk. See page 46.

▲**National Archaeological Museum** Traces the history of Iberia through artifacts, plus a replica of the Altamira Caves. **Hours:** Tue–Sat 9:30–20:00, Sun 9:30–15:00, closed Mon. See page 48.

▲Clothing Museum A clothes look at the 18th–21st centuries. **Hours:** Tue-Sat 9:30–19:00, Sun 10:00–15:00, closed Mon. See page 48.

▲Chapel of San Antonio de la Florida Church with Goya's tomb, plus frescoes by the artist. **Hours:** Tue-Fri 9:30–20:00, Sat-Sun 10:00–14:00, closed Mon. See page 48.

▲El Rastro Europe's biggest flea market. **Hours:** Sun 9:00–15:00, best before 11:00. See page 52.

▲Royal Botanical Garden A relaxing museum of plants, with specimens from around the world. **Hours:** Daily 10:00–21:00, until 18:00 in winter. See page 47.

▲Naval Museum Seafaring history of a country famous for its Armada. **Hours:** Tue-Sun 10:00–14:00, closed Mon and Aug. See page 47.

CaixaForum Impressive exhibit hall with free world-class art exhibits. **Hours:** Daily 10:00–20:00. See page 47.

Descalzas Royal Monastery Working monastery with fine art and tapestries. **Hours:** Tue-Thu and Sat 10:30–12:30 & 16:00–17:30, Fri 10:30–12:30, Sun 11:00–13:30, closed Mon. See page 47.

Sorolla Museum Spanish painter Joaquín Sorrolla's former home and studio. **Hours:** Tue-Sat 9:30–20:00, Sun 10:00–15:00, closed Mon. See page 48.

Municipal Museum Chronicles Madrid's history via paintings, models, and a movie (closed through 2011). See page 48

Royal Tapestry Factory Traditional tapestries woven on site. **Hours:** Mon-Fri 10:00–14:00, closed Sat-Sun and Aug. See page 49.

Temple de Debod Actual ancient Egyptian temple relocated to Madrid. **Hours:** April-Sept Tue-Fri 10:00–14:00 & 18:00–20:00, Sat-Sun 10:00–14:00, closed Mon; Oct-March Tue-Fri 9:45–13:45 & 16:15–18:15, Sat-Sun 10:00–14:00, closed Mon. See page 49.

of Wellington (the general who stopped Napoleon), Stephen founded Madrid's Wellington Society and has been its chairman for over 30 years. For €35, you become a member and get a two-hour tour with a drink and tapas stop (morning or afternoon). His €50 VIP evening tour lasts three hours and includes three stops for drinks and tapas. Eccentric Stephen sorts out Madrid's Habsburg and Bourbon history. He likes his wine—if that's a problem, skip the tour. He also does day trips in the countryside (from €275 per couple; mobile 609-143-203, www.wellsoc.org, chairman@wellsoc.org).

Big-Bus City Sightseeing Tours—Julia Travel offers standard guided bus tours departing from Plaza de España 7 (office open Mon–Fri 8:00–19:00, Sat–Sun 8:00–15:00, tel. 915-599-605). Their city tours include a three-hour Madrid tour with a live guide in two or three languages (€20, one stop for a drink at Hard Rock Café, one shopping stop, no museum visits, daily at 15:00, no reservation required—just show up 15 min before departure). Julia Travel also runs tours to destinations near Madrid. The Valley of the Fallen and El Escorial tour is particularly efficient, given the lousy bus connections for this route (€47, 5 hours, makes the day trip easy—blitzing both sights with a commentary en route and no time-stealing shopping stops, Tue–Sun at 9:00, none Mon). Three trips include Toledo: one of the city itself (€39/5 hours, daily at 9:00 and 15:00, or €52/8 hours, daily at 9:15), one of Madrid and Toledo together (€52, half-day in Toledo plus panoramic 3-hour Madrid tour, daily at 9:00), and a marathon tour of El Escorial, Valley of the Fallen, and Toledo (€95, full day, Tue–Sun at 9:00, none Mon). Note that only the Toledo-only full-day tours include the cathedral. The half-day Toledo and combo-tours skip this town's one must-see sight...but not the long shopping stops, because the shops give kickbacks to the guides.

Self-Guided Walk

Welcome to Madrid:
From the Puerta del Sol to the Royal Palace
Connect the sights with the following commentary. Allow an hour for this half-mile walk. Begin at Madrid's central square, Puerta del Sol (Metro: Sol).

▲▲Puerta del Sol
The bustling Puerta del Sol is named for a long-gone medieval gate with the sun carved onto it. It's a hub for the Metro, buses, political demonstrations, and pickpockets.
• *Stand by the statue of King Charles III and survey the square.*

From Puerta del Sol to the Royal Palace

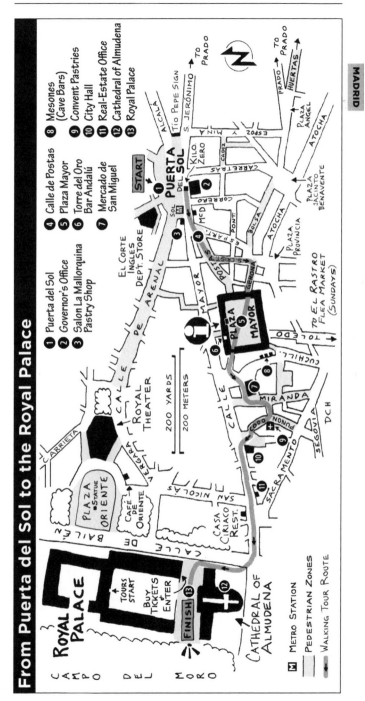

1. Puerta del Sol
2. Governor's Office
3. Salon La Mallorquina Pastry Shop
4. Calle de Postas
5. Plaza Mayor
6. Torre del Oro Bar Andalú
7. Mercado de San Miguel
8. Mesones (Cave Bars)
9. Convent Pastries
10. City Hall
11. Real-Estate Office
12. Cathedral of Almudena
13. Royal Palace

M Metro Station

Pedestrian Zones

Walking Tour Route

Because of his enlightened urban policies, King Charles III (who ruled until 1788) is affectionately called "the best mayor of Madrid." He decorated the city squares with fine fountains, got those meddlesome Jesuits out of city government, established the public school system, mandated underground sewers, made the Retiro a public park rather than a royal retreat, and generally cleaned up Madrid.

Look behind the king. The statue of the bear pawing the berry bush and the *madroño* trees in the big planter boxes are symbols of the city. Bears used to live in the royal hunting grounds outside Madrid. And the *madroño* trees produce a berry that makes the traditional *madroño* liqueur.

The king faces a red-and-white building with a bell tower. This was Madrid's first post office, founded by Charles III in the 1760s. Today, it's the county governor's office, though it's notorious for having been Francisco Franco's police headquarters. An amazing number of those detained and interrogated by the Franco police "tried to escape" by jumping out the windows to their deaths. Notice the hats of the civil guardsmen at the entry. It's said the hats have square backs, cleverly designed so that the men can lean against the wall while enjoying a cigarette.

Appreciate the harmonious architecture of the buildings that circle the square. Crowds fill the square on New Year's Eve as the rest of Madrid watches the action on TV. As Spain's "Big Ben" atop the governor's office chimes 12 times, Madrileños eat one grape for each ring to bring good luck through each of the next 12 months.

• *Cross the square, walking to the governor's office.*

Look at the curb directly in front of the entrance to the **governor's office.** The scuffed-up marker is "kilometer zero," the very center of Spain (with its six main highways indicated). Near the entrance are two plaques expressing thanks from the regional government to its citizens for assisting in times of dire need. To the left of the entrance, a plaque on the wall honors those who helped during the terrorist bombings of March 11, 2004.

A similar plaque on the right marks the spot where the war against Napoleon started in 1808. Napoleon wanted his brother to be king of Spain. Trying to finagle this, he brought nearly the entire Spanish royal family to France for negotiations. An anxious crowd gathered outside this building awaiting word of the fate of their royals. This was just after the French Revolution, and there was a general nervousness between France and Spain. When the people of Madrid heard that Napoleon had appointed his own brother as the new king of Spain, they gathered angrily in the streets. The French guard simply massacred the mob. Painter Francisco de Goya, who worked just up the street, observed the event and captured the tragedy in his paintings *Second of May, 1808* and *Third of May, 1808,* now in the Prado.

From Puerta del Sol to Plaza Mayor

On the corner of Calle Mayor and Puerta del Sol (downhill end of Puerta del Sol, across from McDonald's) is the busy *confitería* **Salon La Mallorquina** (daily 9:00–21:15, closed mid-July–Aug). Go inside for a tempting peek at racks with goodies hot out of the oven. Enjoy observing the churning energy at the bar lined with locals popping in for a fast coffee and a sweet treat. The shop is famous for its cream-filled *Napolitana* pastry (€1). Or sample Madrid's answer to doughnuts, *rosquillas* (*tontas* means "silly"— plain, and *listas* means "all dressed up and ready to go"—with icing, €0.50 each). The room upstairs is more genteel.

From inside the shop, look back toward the entrance and notice the tile above the door with the 18th-century view of Puerta del Sol. Compare this with today's view out the door. This was before the square was widened, when a church stood where the *Tío Pepe* sign stands today. The French used this church to detain local patriots awaiting execution. (The venerable *Tío Pepe* sign, advertising a famous sherry for more than 100 years, was Madrid's first billboard, and today it's the only such ad allowed on the square.)

• *Cross busy Calle Mayor, round McDonald's, and veer up the pedestrian alley called* **Calle de Postas.**

The street sign shows the post coach heading for that famous first post office. Medieval street signs included pictures so the illiterate could "read" them. Fifty yards up the street, at Calle San Cristóbal, is Pans & Company, a popular Catalan sandwich chain. While Spaniards consider American fast food unhealthy—both culturally and physically—the local fast-food chains seem to be more politically and nutritionally correct.

• *From here, hike up Calle San Cristóbal.*

Within two blocks, you'll pass the local feminist bookshop (Librería Mujeres) and reach a small square. At the square, notice the big brick 17th-century Ministry of Foreign Affairs building (with the pointed spire)—originally a jail for aristocratic prisoners, since even the black sheep of fine families were given special treatment.

• *Turn right, and walk down Calle de Zaragoza under the arcade into the...*

▲Plaza Mayor

This square, built in 1619, is a vast cobbled traffic-free chunk of 17th-century Spain. Each side of the square is uniform, as if a grand palace were turned inside-out. The statue is of Philip III, who ordered the square's construction. Before the statue stood here, this site served as the city's theater/multimedia center of the 17th century. Upon this stage, much Spanish history has been played out: bullfights, fires, royal

pageantry, and events of the gruesome Inquisition. Reliefs serving as seatbacks under the lampposts tell the story. During the Inquisition, many were tried here—suspected heretics, Protestants, Jews, tour guides without a local license, and Muslims whose "conversion" to Christianity was dubious. The guilty were paraded around the square before their execution, wearing billboards listing their many sins (bleachers were built for bigger audiences, while the wealthy rented balconies). Some were slowly strangled as they held a crucifix, hearing the reassuring words of a priest as this life was squeezed out of them with a garrote. Others were burned.

The square is painted a democratic shade of burgundy—the result of a citywide vote. Since Franco's death in 1975, there's been a passion for voting here. Three different colors were painted as samples on the walls of this square, and the city voted for its favorite.

A stamp-and-coin market bustles here on Sundays from 10:00 to 14:00; on any day, it's a colorful and affordable place to enjoy a cup of coffee. Throughout Spain, lesser *plazas mayores* provide

peaceful pools in the river of Spanish life. The TI (daily 9:30–20:30, wonderfully air-conditioned and with free but limited Internet access) is under the building on the north side of the square, the Casa de la Panadería, decorated with painted figures (it once housed the Bakers'

Guild). The TI is also a meeting point for cheap daily walking tours—consider dropping by to reserve a spot (see "Tours in Madrid," earlier).

• *For some interesting, if gruesome, bullfighting lore, drop by the...*

Torre del Oro Bar Andalú

This bar is a good spot for a drink to finish off your Plaza Mayor visit (northwest corner of square, to the left of the Bakers' Guild). The bar has *Andalú* (Andalusian) ambience and an entertaining staff. Warning: They push expensive tapas on tourists. But buying a beer is safe and painless—just order a *caña* (small beer, shouldn't cost more than €2.50). The price list posted outside the door makes your costs perfectly clear (*mostrador* indicates the price at the bar).

The interior of the Torre del Oro bar is a temple to bullfighting, festooned with gory decor. Notice the breathtaking action captured in the many photographs. Look under the stuffed head of Barbero the bull. At eye level, you'll see a *puntilla,* the knife used to put a bull out of his misery at the arena. This was the knife used to kill Barbero. The plaque explains: weight, birth date, owner, date of death, which matador killed him, and the location. Just to the left of Barbero, there's a photo of Franco with a very famous bullfighter. This is Manuel Benítez Pérez—better known as El Cordobés, the Elvis of bullfighters and a working-class hero. At the top of the stairs to the WC, find the photo of El Cordobés and Robert Kennedy—looking like brothers. At the end of the bar in a glass case is the "suit of lights" the great El Cordobés wore in his ill-fated 1967 fight. With Franco in attendance, El Cordobés went on and on, long after he could have ended the fight, until finally the bull gored him. El Cordobés survived; the bull didn't. Find another photo of Franco with El Cordobés at the far end, to the left of Segador the bull. Under the bull (to the left, over the counter) is a photo of El Cordobés' illegitimate son kissing a bull. Disowned by El Cordobés senior, yet still using his dad's famous name after a court battle, the new El Cordobés is one of this generation's top fighters.

Consider taking a break at one of their sidewalk tables (or at any café/bar terrace facing Madrid's finest square). Cafetería Margerit (nearby) occupies the sunniest corner of the square and is a good place to enjoy a coffee with the view. The scene is easily worth the extra euro you'll pay for the drink.

Strolling from Plaza Mayor to the Royal Palace

Leave Plaza Mayor on Calle Ciudad Rodrigo (to your right as you exit the bull bar). You'll pass a series of fine turn-of-the-20th-century storefronts and sandwich joints, such as Casa Rúa, famous for their cheap *bocadillos de calamares*—fried squid rings on a roll.

From the archway, you'll see the covered **Mercado de San Miguel** (ornate iron posts, on left). This historic market has morphed into a gourmet food mall.

Before passing the market hall, look left down the street called Cava de San Miguel. If you like sangria and singing, come back after 22:00 and visit one of the *mesones* that line the street. These cave-like bars stretch way back and get packed with locals out on tacky dates who—emboldened by sangria, the setting, and Spain—might suddenly just start singing. It's a lowbrow, electric-keyboard, karaoke-type ambience, best on Friday and Saturday nights. There's a reason for these underground vaults—Plaza Mayor was built on a slope and they are part of a structural system that braces the leveled plaza.

• *On the opposite (downhill) side of the market, follow the pedestrian lane left. At the first corner, turn right and cross the small plaza to the modern brick* **convent.**

Notice the proud coat of arms over the convent's main entry. In Spain, the most prestigious thing a noble family could do was build and maintain a convent. To harvest all the goodwill created in your community, you'd want your family's insignia right there for all to see.

The door on the right says *venta de dulces* (sweets for sale). To buy goodies from the cloistered nuns, buzz the *monjas* button, then wait patiently for the sister to respond over the intercom. Say *"dulces"* (DOOL-thays), and she'll let you in (Mon-Sat 9:30–13:00 & 16:00–18:30, closed Sun). When the lock buzzes, push open the door and follow the sign to *torno,* the lazy Susan that lets the sisters sell their baked goods without being seen (smallest quantity: half, or *medio,* kilo—around €8). Of the many choices listed (all good), *galletas* (shortbread cookies) are the least expensive. The *pastas de almendra* (almond cookies) are a treat.

• *Follow Calle del Codo (where those in need of bits of armor shopped— see the street sign) uphill around the convent to Plaza de la Villa, the square where the* **City Hall** *is located. Stop at the gate before entering the square to notice (on your left) what's considered the oldest door in town on Madrid's oldest building—made of flint and inhabited since 1480.*

Imagine how Philip II took this city by surprise when he decided to move the capital of Europe's largest empire—in the 17th century, even bigger than ancient Rome—from Toledo to humble Madrid. With no great edifices to administer their empire, the Habsburgs went on a building spree. But since their empire was drained of its riches by prolonged religious wars, they built Madrid with brick instead of more expensive and elegant granite.

The statue in the garden is of Don Alvaro de Bazán—mastermind of the Christian victory over the Turkish Ottomans at the naval battle of Lepanto in 1571. This pivotal battle, fought off the coast of Greece, slowed the Turkish threat to Christian Europe. This square was the heart of medieval Madrid, though little remains of the 14th-century town.

From here, busy Calle Mayor leads downhill for a couple more blocks to the Royal Palace. Halfway down (on the left), at #75, a **real-estate office** *(inmobiliaria)* advertises apartments for rent (apartments or condos, priced by the month—are in the hundreds or low thousands of euros) and condos for sale (with six-digit prices). To roughly convert square meters to square feet, multiply by 10. Notice how, for large items, locals still think in terms of *pesetas* ("pts"), the Spanish currency before euros took over in 2002.

A few steps farther down, on a tiny square opposite the recommended Casa Ciriaco restaurant (at #84), a statue memorializes the 1906 anarchist bombing. The target was the royal couple as they paraded by on their wedding day. While the crowd was throwing flowers, an anarchist (what terrorists used to be called) threw a bouquet lashed to a bomb from a balcony of #84, which was a hotel at the time. He missed the royal newlyweds, but killed 23 people. Gory photos of the event hang inside the restaurant (to the right of the entrance).

• *Continue down Calle Mayor. Within a couple of blocks, you'll come to a busy street, Calle de Bailén.*

Across the busy street is Madrid's **Cathedral of Almudena** (built 1883–1993). While it faces the Royal Palace, you'll enter on the side from Calle de Bailén. Before entering (€1 donation requested), notice the central door featuring a relief of the cathedral's 1993 consecration with Pope John Paul II, King Juan Carlos, Queen Sofía, and Princess María Mercedes (the king's mom, in a wheelchair). While the exterior is a contemporary mix, the interior is Neo-Gothic, with a refreshingly modern and colorful ceiling, glittering 5,000-pipe organ, and a fine 15th-century painted altarpiece—striking in the otherwise modern interior. The historic highlight is the 12th-century coffin (empty, painted leather on wood, in a chapel behind the altar) of Madrid's patron saint, Isidro. A humble peasant, Isidro loved the handicapped and performed miracles. Forty years after he died, this coffin was opened and his body was found miraculously preserved, which convinced the pope to canonize him as the patron saint of Madrid and of farmers, with May 15 as his feast day.

Next to the cathedral is the **Royal Palace.** Visit the palace

Cheap Tricks in Madrid

- Instead of expensive city tour buses, take bus #27 on a €1 sightseeing joyride past some major Madrid landmarks. Catch the bus in front of the Royal Botanical Garden on the Paseo del Prado and ride it to the Plaza Castilla (the end of the line). This ride is described later in this chapter, under "Experiences in Madrid."
- Some major sights are free to enter at certain times (for example, the Prado is free Tue-Sat 18:00-20:00 and Sun 17:00-20:00, while the Centro de Arte Reina Sofía is free Sat afternoon after 14:30 and all day Sun). These Madrid sights are always free: CaixaForum, Naval Museum, Chapel of San Antonio de la Florida, Bullfighting Museum, Caja Madrid, and the Temple de Debod.
- The Plaza Mayor TI organizes cheap 90-minute English-language guided walks. Called Discover Madrid, they have different themes, run several times a day, and cost only €4.
- The Plaza Mayor TI has limited free Internet access.

now, using my self-guided tour (see below).

• *When you're finished, you may want to...*

Return to Puerta del Sol

With your back to the palace, face the equestrian statue of Philip IV and (beyond the statue) the Neoclassical **Royal Theater** (Teatro Real, rebuilt in 1997). On your left, the once-impressive **Madrid Tower** skyscraper marks the Plaza de España. Walk behind the Royal Theater (on the right, passing Café de Oriente—a favorite with theater-goers) to another square, where you'll find the Ópera Metro stop and the wonderfully pedestrianized Calle del Arenal, which leads back to Puerta del Sol.

Sights in Madrid

▲▲▲Royal Palace (Palacio Real)

Europe's third-greatest palace (after Versailles and Vienna's Schönbrunn), with arguably the most sumptuous original interior, is packed with tourists and royal antiques.

After a fortress burned down on this site in the 18th century, King Philip V commissioned this huge palace as a replacement. Though he ruled Spain for 40 years, Philip V was very French. (The grandson of Louis XIV, he was born in Versailles and preferred speaking French.) He ordered this palace to be built as his own Versailles (although his wife's Italian origin had a tremendous

impact on the style). It's big—more than 2,000 rooms, with tons of luxurious tapestries, a king's ransom of chandeliers, priceless porcelain, and bronze decor covered in gold leaf. While these days the royal family lives in a mansion a few miles away, this place still functions as a royal palace, and is used for formal state receptions, royal weddings, and tourists' daydreams.

The lions you'll see throughout were symbols of power. The Bourbon kings considered previous royalty not up to European par, and this palace—along with their establishment of a Spanish porcelain works and tapestry works—was their effort to raise the bar.

Cost and Hours: €8 without a tour, €10 with a 60-min tour (explained below); April–Sept Mon–Sat 9:00–19:00, Sun 9:00–16:00; Oct–March Mon–Sat 9:30–18:00, Sun 9:00–15:00; last entry one hour before closing. The palace can close if needed for a royal function; you can call a day ahead to check (tel. 914-548-800).

Crowd-Beating Tips: The palace is most crowded on Wednesdays, when it's free for locals. To minimize lines, either arrive early, or go late any day except Wednesday.

Getting There: To get to the palace from Puerta del Sol, walk down the pedestrianized Calle del Arenal. If arriving by Metro, get off at the Ópera stop.

Services: At the palace, there are free lockers and a WC just past the ticket booth. Upstairs, you'll find a fine air-conditioned cafeteria (with salad bar) and a more serious bookstore.

Touring the Palace: A simple one-floor, 24-room one-way circuit is open to the public. You can wander on your own or join an English-language tour (check time of next tour and decide as you buy your ticket; the English-language tours depart sporadically, not worth a long wait). The tour guides, like the museum guidebook, show a passion for meaningless data. The €2.30 audioguides are much more interesting, and they complement what I describe below. If you enjoy sightseeing cheek-to-cheek, crank up the volume and share the audioguide with your companion. The armory and the pharmacy (included in your ticket) are in the courtyard. Photography is not allowed.

➲ **Self-Guided Tour:** If you tour the palace on your own, here are a few details beyond what you'll find on the little English descriptions posted in each room.

1. The Palace Lobby: In the old days, horse-drawn carriages would drop you off here. Today, limos for gala events do the same thing. Look for a sign that divides the visitors waiting for a tour from those going in alone. The modern black bust in the corner is of the current, very popular constitutional monarch—King Juan Carlos I. He's a "peoples' king," credited with bringing democracy to Spain after Franco.

2. The Grand Stairs: Fancy carpets are rolled down (notice the little metal bar-holding hooks) for formal occasions. At the top

of the first landing, the blue-and-red coat of arms represents Juan Carlos. While Franco chose him to be his successor, J. C. knew Spain was ripe for democracy. Rather than become "Juan the Brief" (as some were nicknaming him), he turned real power over to the parliament. You'll see his (figure) head on the back of the Spanish €1 and €2 coins. At the top of the stairs (before entering first room, right of door) is a white marble bust of J. C.'s great-great-g-g-g-great-grandfather Philip V, who began the Bourbon dynasty in Spain in 1700 and had this palace built.

3. Guard Room: The palace guards used to hang out in this relatively simple room. Notice the fine clocks. Charles IV, a great collector, amassed more than 700. The 150 clocks displayed in this palace are all in working order. Look up, and see the first ceiling fresco in a series by the great Venetian painter Giambattista (or G. B.) Tiepolo (also see "Throne Room," below). Most of what you see in the palace dates from the 18th century. But the carpet in this room was made in 1991 (see the corner folded over). While modern, it's made the traditional way—by hand in Madrid's royal tapestry factory.

4. Hall of Columns: Originally a ballroom and dining room, today this space is used for formal ceremonies. (For example, this is where Spain formally joined the European Union in 1985—see plaque on far wall.) The tapestries (like most you'll see in the palace) are 17th-century Belgian, from designs by Raphael. The central theme in the ceiling fresco is Apollo driving the chariot of the sun, while Bacchus enjoys wine, women, and song with a convivial gang. This is a reminder that the mark of a good king is to drive the chariot of state as smartly as Apollo, while providing an environment where the people can enjoy life to the fullest.

5. Throne Room: Red velvet walls, lions, and frescoes of Spanish scenes symbolize the monarchy in this Rococo riot. The 12 mirrors, impressive in their day, each represent a different month. The chandeliers (silver and crystal from Murano near Venice) are the best in the house. While the room is decorated in the 18th-century style, the throne dates only from 1977. In Spain, a new one is built for each king or queen (with a gilded portrait on the back). This is where the king's guests salute Juan Carlos before dinner. He receives them relatively informally...standing at floor level, rather than seated up on the throne. The coat of arms above the throne shows the complexity of the Bourbon empire across Europe—which, in the 18th century, included Tirol, Sicily, Burgundy, the Netherlands, and more.

The ceiling fresco (1764) is the last great work by Italian master G. B. Tiepolo, who died in Madrid in 1770. This painting celebrates the days of the vast Spanish empire—upon which the sun also never set. Find the Native American (hint: follow the rainbow to the macho red-caped conquistador who motions to someone he conquered).

The next several rooms were the living quarters of King Charles III (ruled 1759–1788). After his lunch room (with the round sofa in the center), you come to the...

6. Antechamber: The four paintings are of King Charles IV (looking a bit like a dim-witted George Washington) and his wife, María Luisa (who wore the pants in the palace)—all originals by Francisco de Goya. To meet the demand for his work, he made copies of these (which you'll see in the Prado). The clock—showing Cronus, god of time, in porcelain, bronze, and mahogany—sits on a music box. The gilded decor you see throughout the palace is bronze with gold leaf. Velázquez's famous painting *Las Meninas* (which you'll marvel at in the Prado) originally hung in this room.

7. Gasparini Room: This was meant to be Charles III's bedroom, but wasn't finished when he died. Instead, with its painted stucco ceiling and inlaid Spanish marble floor, it was the royal dressing room. It's a triumph of the Rococo style, with exotic motifs that were in vogue during that period. The Asian influence, also trendy at the time, is clear in the corners of the ornate ceiling. During restoration in 1992, the silk wallpaper was replaced with the original embroidery. Note the fine micro-mosaic table—a typical royal or aristocratic souvenir from any visit to Rome in the mid-1800s. For a divine monarch, dressing was a public affair. The court bigwigs would assemble here as the king, standing on a platform—notice the height of the mirrors—would pull on his leotards and toy with his wig.

In the next room, the silk wallpaper is new (*J.C.S.* indicates King Juan Carlos and Queen Sofía).

• *Pass through the silk room to reach...*

8. Charles III Bedroom: This room is dedicated to Charles III, known as one of the enlightened monarchs, who died here in his bed in 1788. His grandson, Ferdinand VII, commissioned the fresco on the ceiling, showing thanks to God for the birth of the first male grandson (that would be Ferdy himself) to continue the dynasty. Decorated in 19th-century Neoclassical style, the chandelier is in the shape of the fleur-de-lis (symbol of the Bourbon family) capped with a Spanish crown. The thick walls separating each room hide service corridors for servants, who scurried about generally unseen.

9. Porcelain Room: The several hundred plates that line this room were disassembled for safety during the Spanish Civil War. (Find the little screws in the greenery that hide the seams.)

The Neoclassical Yellow Room was a study for Charles III. Notice the fine chandelier, with properly cut crystal that shows all the colors of the rainbow.

10. Gala Dining Room: Up to 12 times a year, the king entertains as many as 144 guests at this bowling lane–size table, which can be extended to the length of the room. Find the two royal chairs. (Hint: With the modesty necessary for 21st-century monarchs, they are only a tad higher than the rest.) The parquet floor was the preferred dancing surface when balls were held in this fabulous room. Note the vases from China and the fresco depicting Christopher Columbus with exotic souvenirs and new, red-skinned friends. Imagine the lighting when the 15 chandeliers (and their 900 bulbs) are fired up.

11. Cinema Room (Sala de Monedas y Medallas): In the early 20th century, the royal family enjoyed "Sunday afternoons at the movies" here. Today, this room stores glass cases filled with coins and medals. The table used to be set up with lavish bouquets of flowers and fruits, which ended up in the dining room as centerpieces, effectively making it impossible for guests to talk across the table.

12. Silver Room: This collection of silver tableware dates from the 19th century. The older royal silver was melted down by Napoleon's brother to help fund wars of the Napoleonic age. If you look carefully, you can see quirky royal necessities, including a baby's silver rattle.

13. China Rooms: Several collections of china from different kings (some actually from China, others from royal workshops in Europe such as Sèvres and Meissen) are displayed in this room. This room illustrates how any self-respecting royal family in Europe would have had its own porcelain works (the technique was a royal secret).

• *Exit to the hallway and notice the interior courtyard you've been circling one room at a time. You can see how the royal family lived in the spacious middle floor while staff was upstairs, and the kitchens, garage, and storerooms were on the ground level. Between statues of the giants of Spanish royal history (Isabel and Ferdinand), you'll enter the...*

14. Royal Chapel: This chapel (likely closed for restoration in 2010) is used for private concerts and funerals. The royal coffin sits here before making the sad trip to El Escorial to join the rest of Spain's past royalty (see next chapter).

15. Queen's Boudoir: This room was for the ladies.

16. Stradivarius Room: The queen likes classical music. When you perform for her, do it with these precious 350-year-old violins. Of all of the instruments Antonius Stradivarius made, only 300 survive. This is the only matching quartet: two violins, a viola, and a cello.

17. Billiards and Smoking Rooms: The billiards room (with its English men's-club paneling) and the adjacent smoking room were for men only. The porcelain and silk of the smoking room imitates a Chinese opium den, which, in its day, was furnished only with pillows.

18. Queen's Tearoom: Small and intimate, the Neoclassical Wedgwood-like decoration stands out.

19. Fine Woods Room: Fine 18th- and 19th-century French inlaid-wood pieces decorate this room.

Exit the palace down the same grand stairway you climbed 24 rooms ago. Cross the big courtyard, heading to the far right corner to the...

20. Armory: Here you'll find the armor and swords of Ferdinand (husband of Isabel), Charles V (ruler of Spain at its peak of power), and Philip II (Charles' son, who watched Spain start its long slide downward).

Just inside the entry, you'll see the oldest piece in the collection: the shield of Boabdil, the last Moorish king who surrendered Granada in 1492. This main room is dominated by the armor of Charles V and Philip II—who dominated Europe in the 16th century. At the far end you'll meet Charles V on horseback. The mannequin of the king wears the same armor and assumes the same pose made famous by Titian's painting.

The tapestry above the armor warmed the walls of the otherwise stark palace that predated this one. Tapestries traveled ahead of royals to decorate their living space. They made many palaces "fit for a king" back when the only way to effectively govern was to be on the road a lot.

Circle the big room clockwise. The long wall on the left displays the armor of Charles V. The opposite wall showcases the armor and weapons of Philip II. Philip, who impoverished Spain with his wars against the Protestants, anticipated that debt collectors would ransack his estate after his death and specifically protected his fine collection of armor.

Downstairs is more armor, a mixed collection mostly from the 17th century. Notice the life-saving breastplates dimpled with bullet dents before you leave (to right of exit door).

Climb the steps from the armory exit to the viewpoint. This

vast palace backyard, today a city park, was the king's hunting ground.

21. Pharmacy: The royal pharmacy is opposite the armory, near the entry. Wander through six rooms stacked with jars and jugs of herbal cures, past exotic beakers, and under portraits of royal doctors with good English descriptions explaining 18th- and 19th-century medicine.

The upstairs, above the exit, has an air-conditioned cafeteria and a bookstore, which has a good variety of books on Spanish history. As you leave the palace, walk around the corner to the left, along the palace exterior, to the grand yet people-friendly Plaza de Oriente (with my recommended lunch spot, Café de Oriente; wonderful €13 lunch special, Mon-Fri 13:00-16:00). Throughout Europe, energetic governments are turning formerly car-congested wastelands into public spaces like this. Madrid's last mayor was nicknamed "The Mole" for all the digging he did. Where's all the traffic? Under your feet.

Madrid's Museum Neighborhood

Three great museums, all within a 10-minute walk of each other, cluster in east Madrid: El Prado (Europe's top collection of paintings), the Thyssen-Bornemisza Museum (a baron's collection of European art, from the old masters to the moderns), and the Centro de Arte Reina Sofía (modern art, including Picasso's famous *Guernica*).

If visiting all three museums, save a few euros by buying the ***Paseo del Arte*** combo-ticket (€14.40, buy at any of the three museums, good for a year). Note that it's free to enter the Prado Tuesday–Saturday 18:00–20:00, and Sunday 17:00–20:00, and the Reina Sofía Saturday 14:30–21:00 and Sunday 10:00–14:30 (both are free anytime for those under 18). The Prado and Thyssen-Bornemisza are closed Monday, and the Reina Sofía is closed Tuesday.

▲▲▲Prado Museum

With more than 3,000 canvases, including entire rooms of masterpieces by superstar painters, the Prado (PRAH-doh) is overwhelming. But if you use the free English floor plan (pick up as you enter) and follow my self-guided tour (see below), you'll be impressed. The Prado is *the* place to enjoy the great Spanish painter Francisco de Goya, and it's also the home of Diego Velázquez's *Las Meninas*, considered by many to be the world's finest painting, period. In addition to Spanish works,

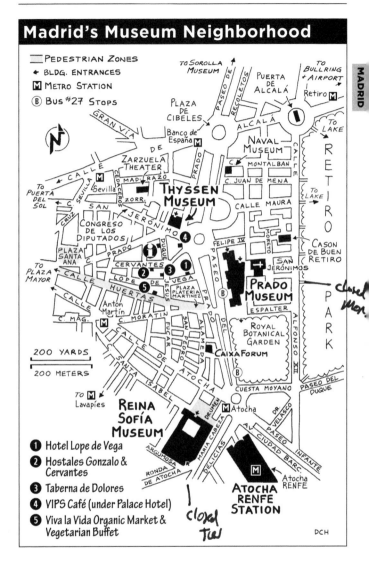

Madrid's Museum Neighborhood

PEDESTRIAN ZONES
- BLDG. ENTRANCES
- Ⓜ METRO STATION
- Ⓑ BUS #27 STOPS

MADRID

Map labels: TO SOROLLA MUSEUM, TO BULLRING & AIRPORT, PUERTA DE ALCALÁ, PLAZA DE CIBELES, Retiro Ⓜ, TO LAKE, Banco de España Ⓜ, GRAN VIA, NAVAL MUSEUM, ALCALÁ, MONTALBAN, C. JUAN DE MENA, ZARZUELA THEATER, MAD. RAZO, Sevilla, THYSSEN MUSEUM, CALLE MAURA, RETIRO, TO PUERTA DEL SOL, ZORR., SAN, CONGRESO DE LOS DIPUTADOS, JERONIMO, FELIPE IV, SAN JERÓNIMOS, CASON DE BUEN RETIRO, PLAZA SANTA ANA, PRADO, CERVANTES, DUQUE, PRADO MUSEUM, TO PLAZA MAYOR, LOPE DE VEGA, PLAZA PLATERÍA MARTÍNEZ, ESPALTER, HUERTAS, JESUS, Anton Martin, C. MORATIN, ROYAL BOTANICAL GARDEN, P A R K, C. MAG., FUCAR, CAIXAFORUM, ALFONSO XII, 200 YARDS, 200 METERS, SANTA, ISABEL, ATOCHA, CUESTA MOYANO, PASEO DEL DUQUE, TO Ⓜ Lavapiés, REINA SOFÍA MUSEUM, DRUMEN, MARIA CABEZA, Ⓜ Atocha, DR. VELASCO, ARGUMOSA, DELICIAS, AV. CIUDAD BARC., PASEO INFANTE, RONDA DE ATOCHA, Ⓜ, ATOCHA RENFE STATION, Atocha RENFE, DCH

1. Hotel Lope de Vega
2. Hostales Gonzalo & Cervantes
3. Taberna de Dolores
4. VIPS Café (under Palace Hotel)
5. Viva la Vida Organic Market & Vegetarian Buffet

(handwritten notes: "closed Mon", "closed Tue")

---

you'll find paintings by Italian and Flemish masters, including Hieronymus Bosch's delightful *Garden of Delights* altarpiece.

Cost and Hours: €6, free Tue–Sat 18:00–20:00 and Sun 17:00–20:00, and free anytime to anyone under 18. Open Tue–Sun 9:00–20:00, closed Mon, last entry 30 min before closing.

Location: It's at the Paseo del Prado. The Banco de España (line 2) and Atocha Metro (line 1) stops are each a five-minute walk from the museum.

The Prado Expansion: The first extension, inaugurated in

2007, was partially constructed in the cloister of the 17th-century San Jerónimos church. This spacious addition houses a sculpture gallery and temporary exhibits, as well as a café and gift shop. The adjacent army museum is moving to Toledo, which will open up space for sculpture and decorative arts.

Crowd-Beating Tips: Lunchtime (14:00–16:00) and weekdays are generally less crowded. It's always packed when free and on weekends; it's worth paying the entry price on other days to have your space. Free tickets are issued only after 18:00.

Entrances: You can buy your ticket at the Goya entrance. From the ticket office, go around the corner to the left and into the big service-filled Jerónimos entrance. (The Murillo entrance, the one across from the Royal Botanical Garden, is for advance bookings such as school groups.) Pick up a detailed map and consider renting an audioguide.

Tours: Take a tour, rent the €3 audioguide, buy a guidebook, or use my self-guided commentary (next). Given the ever-changing locations of paintings (making my self-guided tour tough to follow), the audioguide (with 120 paintings described) is a good investment, allowing you to wander. When you see a painting of interest, simply punch in the number and enjoy the description. You can return the audioguide at any of the exits. And, if you're on a tight budget, remember that two can crank up the volume, listen cheek-to-cheek, and share one machine.

Services and Information: Your bags will be scanned (just like at the airport) before you leave them at the free and mandatory baggage storage (no water bottles, food, backpacks, or large umbrellas allowed inside). A cafeteria is in the extension area near the Jerónimos entrance. Tel. 913-302-800, http://museoprado .mcu.es.

Photography: Not allowed.

❍ Self-Guided Tour: Thanks to Gene Openshaw for writing the following tour.

New World gold funded the Prado, the greatest painting museum in the world. You'll see world-class Italian Renaissance art (especially Titian), Northern art (Bosch, Rubens, Dürer), and Spanish art (El Greco, Velázquez, and Goya). This huge museum is not laid out chronologically, so this tour will not be chronological. Instead, we'll hit the highlights with a minimum of walking. Make sure to have a map (free, available at entry). If you can't find a particular painting, ask a guard.

• *Start at the Room of the Muses (Sala de los Muses), the center of the*

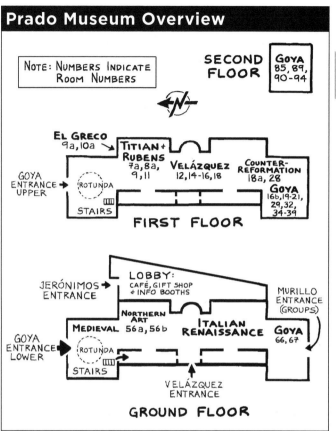

Prado Museum Overview

Note: Numbers Indicate Room Numbers

SECOND FLOOR — Goya 85, 89, 90-94

MADRID

FIRST FLOOR

El Greco 9a, 10a

Titian + Rubens 7a, 8a, 9, 11

Velázquez 12, 14-16, 18

Counter-Reformation 18a, 28

Goya 16b, 19-21, 29, 32, 34-39

Goya Entrance Upper

Rotunda

Stairs

GROUND FLOOR

Jerónimos Entrance

Lobby: Café, Gift Shop & Info Booths

Murillo Entrance (Groups)

Northern Art

Medieval 56a, 56b

Italian Renaissance

Goya 66, 67

Goya Entrance Lower

Rotunda

Stairs

Velázquez Entrance

building. *Go upstairs to the main gallery, filled with Golden Age Spanish art. Go right past the Spanish masters. At the far end of the hall, find Murillo, Rooms 28 and 29.*

Bartolomeo Murillo's *Immaculate Conception (La Inmaculada "de El Escorial")* puts a human face on the abstract Catholic doctrine that Mary was conceived and born free of original sin. Floating in a cloud of Ivory Soap purity, this "immaculate" virgin radiates youth and wholesome goodness.

• *At the far end of the gallery, go into the round Room 32 where you'll see many royal portraits by Goya.*

Francisco de Goya (1746–1828): Follow this complex man through the stages of his life—from dutiful court painter, to political rebel and scandal-maker, to the disillusioned genius of his "dark paintings."

The Family of Charles IV (La Familia de Carlos IV) is all decked out in their Sunday best for this group portrait. Goya himself

MADRID

stands to the far left, painting the court (a tribute to Velázquez in *Las Meninas*)...and revealing the shallow people beneath the royal trappings. King Charles, with his ridiculous hairpiece and goofy smile, was a vacuous, henpecked husband. His domineering queen upstages him, arrogantly stretching her swan-

like neck. The other adults, with their bland faces, are bug-eyed with stupidity.

• *Find the staircase or elevator behind* The Family of Charles IV *and head up to the second floor.*

Rooms 90–94 display canvases that were Goya's designs to make tapestries for nobles' palaces. The scenes make it clear that,

while revolution was brewing in America and France, Spain's lords and ladies played—picnicking, dancing, flying kites, playing paddleball and Blind Man's Bluff, or just relaxing in the sun—the well-known *The Parasol (El Quitasol)* is in Room 85.

• *Return down the stairs to the first floor, Room 36.*

Rumors flew that Goya was fooling around with the vivacious Duchess of Alba, and he may have painted her in a scandalous pose. You'll find two similar paintings, the *Nude Maja (La Maja Desnuda)* and *Clothed Maja (La Maja Vestida)*. A *maja* was the name for a trendy, working-class girl. Whether she's a duchess or a *maja*, Goya had painted a naked lady. And

that was enough to risk incurring the wrath of the Inquisition. The *Nude* stretches in a Titian-esque pose to display her charms, the pale body highlighted by cool green sheets. According to a believable legend, the two paintings were displayed in a double frame, with the *Clothed Maja* sliding over the front to hide the *Nude* from Inquisitive minds.

• *Go back by the stairs still on the first floor, Room 39.*

Goya became a political liberal, a champion of democracy. He was crushed when France's hero of the Revolution, Napoleon,

morphed into a tyrant and invaded Spain. On the *Second of May, 1808*, Madrid's citizens were protesting the occupation in Puerta del Sol, when the French sent in their dreaded Egyptian mercenaries. They plow through the dense tangle of Madrileños, who have nowhere to run. The next day, the *Third of May, 1808,* the French rounded up ringleaders and executed them. The colorless firing squad—a faceless machine of death—mows them down, and they fall in bloody, tangled heaps. Goya throws a harsh prison-yard floodlight on the main victim, who spreads his arms Christ-like to ask, "Why?"

Politically, Goya was split—he was a Spaniard but he knew France was leading Europe into the modern age. His art, while political, has no Spanish or French flags. It's a universal comment on the horror of war. Many consider Goya the last classical and first modern painter...the first painter with a social conscience.

• *To find the "dark paintings," silently flagellate yourself, then go downstairs to Rooms 66 and 67.*

The Colossus shows the destitution following the war with France. This was the world as Goya saw it. Depressed and deaf from syphilis, he retired to his small home and smeared the walls with his "dark paintings"...dark in color and in mood. From this point until his death, Goya would paint his nightmares...literally. The style is considered Romantic—emphasizing emotion over beauty—but it foreshadows 20th-century Surrealism with its bizarre imagery and Expressionism, thick brushstrokes and cynical outlook.

Stepping into Room 67 you are surrounded by art from Goya's dark period. He painted what he felt with a radical technique not burdened with reality—a century before his time. And he painted without being paid for it. This room contains, I believe, the first rare art done without a commission.

Dark forces convened continually in Goya's dining room, where *The Witches' Sabbath (El Aquelarre)* hung. The witches, who look like skeletons, swirl in a frenzy around a dark, Satanic goat in monk's clothing who presides over the obscene rituals. The main witch exudes wild-eyed adoration and lust, while a noble lady (right of center) folds her hands primly in her lap ("I thought this was a Tupperware party!"). Or, perhaps it's a pep rally for her execution, maybe inspired by the excited frenzy that accompanied Plaza Mayor executions. Nobody knows for sure.

In the *Battle to the Death (Duelo a Garrotazos),* two giants stand face to face, buried up to their knees, and flail at each other with clubs. It's a standoff between superpowers in the never-ending cycle of war—a vision of a tough time when people on the streets would kill for a piece of bread.

In *Saturn Devouring One of His Sons (Saturno)*, we see Saturn—fearful that his sons would overthrow him as king of the Roman gods—eating one of them. Saturn, also known as Cronus (Time), may symbolize how time devours us all. (Either way, the painting brings new meaning to the term "child's portion.")

The Dog (El Perro) is, according to some, the hinge between classic art and modern art. The dog, so full of feeling and sadness, is being swallowed by quicksand...much as, to Goya, the modern age was overtaking a more classical era.

• *Go back upstairs into Room 18a.*

Spanish Counter-Reformation Art: In the 1600s, when Europe was torn between Protestant and Catholic ideologies, devoted Spanish artists used images to bolster the Catholic faithful and explain abstract church doctrines. So Francisco Zurbarán's *St. Peter Crucified Appearing to Peter Nolasco (Aparición de San Pedro a San Pedro Nolasco)* renders the mystical vision absolutely literally. Bam, there's the Apostle Peter on an upside-down cross right in front of us. Nolasco looks as shocked as we'd be.

• *Velázquez can be found in Rooms 18 and 16–14, with a grand finale in large lozenge-shaped Room 12.*

Diego Velázquez (1599–1660): Velázquez (vel-LAHTH-keth) was the photojournalist of court painters, capturing the Spanish king and his court with a blend of formal portrait and candid snapshot.

Prince Balthazar Carlos on Horseback (El Príncipe Baltasar Carlos, a Caballo) is exactly the kind of portrait Velázquez was called on to produce. The prince prances like a Roman emperor—only this "emperor" is just a cute little five-year-old acting oh so serious. Get up close and notice that his remarkably detailed costume is nothing but a few messy splotches of pink and gold paint—the proto-Impressionism Velázquez helped pioneer.

The Surrender of Breda (La Rendición de Breda) is a piece of artistic journalism, chronicling Spain's victory over the Dutch. The defeated Dutchman starts to kneel, but the Spaniard stops him—no need to rub salt in the wound. Twenty-five lances silhouetted against the sky reinforce the optimistic calm-after-the-battle mood.

Velázquez's boss, King Philip IV, had an affair, got caught, and repented by commissioning the *Crucifixion (Cristo Crucificado)*.

Christ hangs his head, humbly accepting his punishment, while Philip is left to stare at the slowly dripping blood, contemplating how long Christ had to suffer to atone for Philip's sins.

Velázquez's *The Maids of Honor (Las Meninas)* is a peek at nannies caring for Princess Margarita and, at the same time, a behind-the-scenes look at Velázquez at work. One hot summer day in 1656, Velázquez (at left, with paintbrush and Dalí moustache) stands at his easel and stares out at the people he's painting—the king and queen. They would have been standing about where we are, and we see only their reflection in the mirror at the back of the room. Their daughter (blonde hair, in center) watches her parents being painted, joined by her servants *(meninas)*, dwarfs, and the family dog. Also, at that very moment, a man happens to pass by the doorway at back and pauses to look in.

This frozen moment is lit by the window on the right, splitting the room into bright and shaded planes that recede into the distance. The main characters look right at us, making us part of the scene, seemingly able to walk around, behind, and among the characters.

If you stand in the center of the room, the 3-D effect is most striking. This is art come to life. Now look around and see how Velázquez enjoyed capturing light—and capturing the moment.

Velázquez's *The Drinkers (Los Borrachos)* is a cell-phone snapshot in a blue-collar bar, with a couple of peasants mugging for a photo-op with a Greek god—Bacchus, the god of wine. This was an early work, before he got his court-painter gig. A personal homage to the hardworking farmers enjoying the fruit of their labor, it shows how Velázquez had a heart for real people and believed they deserved portraits, too.

• *To find works by Titian, you will need to visit several rooms (Room 11, 7a, 8a). Start in Room 11.*

Titian (c. 1490–1576): Titian painted portraits of Spain's two Golden Age kings—both staunch Catholics—who amassed this racy collection. *Charles V on Horseback (El Emperador Carlos V en la Batalla de Muhlberg,* Room 11) rears on his horse, raises his lance, and rides out to crush an army of Lutherans. Charles, having inherited many kingdoms and baronies through his family connections, was the world's most powerful man in the 1500s.

• *Sitting amid the Titian collection (in Room 9) are works by Rubens, described below. But for now, we'll continue with Titian in Room 8a.*

Danae and the Shower of Gold (Danae Recibiendo la Lluvia de Oro), from Greek mythology, shows the princess opening her legs to receive Zeus, the lecherous king of the gods, who descends as a shower of gold. Danae is helpless with rapture, while her servant tries to catch the holy spurt with a towel.

In contrast, Charles V's son, *Philip II (Felipe II),* looks pale, suspicious, and lonely—a scholarly and complex figure. He built the austere, monastic palace at El Escorial, but also indulged himself with Titian's bevy of Renaissance Playmates—a sampling of which is here in the Prado.

• *Now backtrack to Room 9 to see more flesh.*

Peter Paul Rubens (1577–1640): A native of Flanders, Rubens painted Baroque-style art meant to play on the emotions, titillate the senses, and carry you away. *Diana and Her Nymphs Discovered by a Satyr (Diana y sus Ninfas Sorprendidas por Sátiros)* ripples from left to right with a wave of figures, as the nymphs flee from the half-human sex predators. But Diana, queen of the hunt, turns to

bravely face the satyrs with her spear. All of Rubens' trademarks are here—sex, violence, action, emotion, bright colors, fleshy bodies—with the wind-machine set on 10.

Rubens' *The Three Graces (Las Tres Gracias)* celebrate cellulite. Their ample, glowing bodies intertwine as they exchange meaningful glances. The Grace at left is Rubens' young second wife, who shows up fairly regularly in his paintings.

• *El Greco's works are nearby, in Rooms 9a and 10a.*

El Greco (1541–1614): El Greco was born in Greece (his name is Spanish for "The Greek"), trained in Venice, then settled in Toledo—60 miles from Madrid. His paintings are like Byzantine icons drenched in Venetian color and fused in the fires of Spanish mysticism.

In *Christ Carrying the Cross (Cristo Abrazado a la Cruz)*, Jesus accepts his fate, trudging toward death with blood running down his neck. He hugs the cross and directs his gaze along the crossbar. His upturned eyes (sparkling with a streak of white paint) lock onto his next stop—heaven.

The Adoration of the Shepherds (La Adoración de los Pastores), originally painted for El Greco's own burial chapel in Toledo, has the artist's typical two-tiered composition—heaven above, earth below. The long, skinny shepherds are stretched unnaturally in between, flickering like flames toward heaven.

The Nobleman with His Hand on His Chest (El Caballero de la Mano al Pecho) is an elegant and somewhat arrogant man whose hand has the middle fingers touching—El Greco's trademark way of expressing elegance (or was it the 16th-century symbol for "Live long and prosper"?). The signature is on the right in faint Greek letters—"Doménikos Theotokópoulos," El Greco's real name.

• *Say hello one more time to* Las Meninas *on the way to the stairs and elevator off Room 14. Then go down to the ground floor.*

Italian Renaissance: During its Golden Age (the 1500s), Spain may have been Europe's richest country, but Italy was still the most cultured. Spain's kings loved how Italian Renaissance artists captured a three-dimensional world on a two-dimensional canvas, bringing Bible scenes to life and celebrating real people and their emotions.

Raphael's *Christ Falls on the Way to Calvary (Caida en el Camino del Calvario)* is a study in contrasts. Below the crossbar, Christ and the women swirl in agonized passion. Above, bored soldiers mill about on the bleak hill where Jesus will die.

In the *Death of the Virgin (El Transito de la Virgen)*, Mantegna masters Renaissance 3-D. The apostles mourn in a crowded room, while the floor tiles recede into the distance, creating the subconscious effect of carrying Mary's soul out the window into the serene distance.

Fra Angelico's *The Annunciation (La Anunciación)* is half medieval piety, half Renaissance realism. In the crude Garden of Eden scene (on the left), a scrawny, sinful First Couple hovers unreal-

istically above the foliage, awaiting eviction. The angel's Annunciation to Mary (right side) is more Renaissance, both with its upbeat message (that Jesus will be born to redeem sinners like Adam and Eve) and in the budding photorealism, set beneath 3-D arches. (Still, aren't the receding bars of the porch's ceiling a bit off? Painting three dimensions wasn't that easy.)
• *Go to Room 50.*

Here you'll find Spain's medieval roots. This art features nothing but saints and Bible scenes—appropriate for a country whose extreme religious devotion was forged in seven centuries of bloody war against Muslims.
• *Backtrack to Room 49, take a left through 57b, then through 57, turn left into 58 to see...*

Northern Art: *The Descent from the Cross (El Descendimiento de la Cruz)* is a masterpiece by Flemish painter Roger van der Weyden, showing the psychological character of real people in a contemporary (1435) scene to portray this Biblical event. The Flemish were masters of detail, as you can see in the cloth, jewels, faces, and even tears. The creative composition suggests that, in losing her son, Mary suffered along with Jesus. As the Netherlands was then a part of the Spanish empire, this painting ended up in Madrid.
• *Next, go from Room 58a to 56a to see Bosch's* Garden of Earthly Delights.

Hieronymous Bosch (c. 1450–1516), in his cryptic triptych *The Garden of Earthly Delights (El Jardín de las Delicias)*, relates the message that the pleasures of life are fleeting, so we'd better avoid them or we'll wind up in hell. The large altarpiece has so many

interesting small figures that it helps to "frame off" small sections to catch the details. Here's the big picture: In the central panel, men on horseback ride round and round, searching for but never reaching the elusive Fountain of Youth. Others frolic in earth's "Garden," oblivious to where they came from (paradise, left panel) and where they may end up (hell, right panel). On the left, innocent Adam and Eve get married, with God himself performing the ceremony. The

right panel is hell, a burning wasteland where genetic-mutant demons torture sinners. Everyone gets their just desserts, like the glutton who is eaten and re-eaten eternally. In the center, hell is literally frozen over. A creature with a broken eggshell body, tree-trunk legs, and a witch's cap stares out—it's the face of Bosch himself. Many other fascinating *El Boscos* are in this room.

On the opposite wall, Pieter Bruegel (BROY-gull) the Elder's work chronicles the 16th century's violent Catholic-Protestant wars in *The Triumph of Death (El Triunfo de la Muerte)*. The painting is one big, chaotic battle, featuring skeletons attacking helpless mortals. Bruegel's message is simple and morbid: No one can escape death.

• *Find Dürer's work nearby, in Room 55b.*

Albrecht Dürer's *Self-Portrait (Autorretrato)* is possibly the

first true self-portrait. The artist, age 26, is dolled up in a fancy Italian hat and permed hair. He'd recently returned from Italy and wanted to impress his fellow Germans with his sophistication. But Dürer wasn't simply vain. He'd grown accustomed, as an artist in Renaissance Italy, to being treated like a prince. Note Dürer's signature, the pyramid-shaped "A. D." (D inside the A) on the windowsill.

Dürer's *Adam and Eve* (two separate panels) are the first full-size nudes in Northern European art. Like Greek statues, they pose in their separate niches, with three-dimensional, anatomically correct bodies. This was a bold humanist proclamation that the body is good, man is good, and the things of the world are good.

• *The Prado is also good, but our tour is over. Exit through Room 55 and continue through the red-painted walls to the bright and open space of the Prado extension, where you'll find the café, exhibit halls of the San Jerónimos cloister, and the Jerónimos exit.*

▲▲Thyssen-Bornemisza Museum

Locals call this stunning museum simply the Thyssen (TEE-sun). It displays the impressive collection that Baron Thyssen (a wealthy German married to a former Miss Spain) sold to Spain for $350 million. The museum offers a unique chance to enjoy the sweep of all art history—including a good sampling of the "isms" of the 20th century—in one collection. It's basically minor works by major artists and major works by minor artists. (Major works by major artists are in the Prado.) But art-lovers appreciate how the good baron's art complements the Prado's collection by filling in where the Prado is weak—such as Impressionism, which is the Thyssen's forte.

Cost and Hours: €6 (up to €5 more for optional special exhibits); children under 12 free, Tue–Sun 10:00–19:00, closed Mon, last entry 30 min before closing.

Location: The museum is kitty-corner from the Prado at Paseo del Prado 8 in Palacio de Villahermosa (Metro: Banco de España).

Services and Information: Free baggage storage, €4 audioguide, café, shop, no photos, tel. 914-203-944, www.museo thyssen.org.

Touring the Museum: After purchasing your ticket, continue down the wide main hall past larger-than-life paintings of King Juan Carlos and Queen Sofía, and then paintings of the baron (who died in 2002) and his art-collecting baroness, Carmen. At the info desk, pick up two museum maps (one for numbered rooms, another for lettered rooms): Each floor is divided into two separate areas: the permanent collection (blue-numbered rooms) and additions from the baroness since the 1980s (red-lettered rooms). Most visitors stick to the permanent collection.

Ascend to the top floor and work your way down, taking a delightful walk through art history. Visit the rooms on each floor in numerical order, from Primitive Italian (Room 1) to Surrealism and Pop Art (Room 48).

Temporary exhibits at the Thyssen often parallel those at the free **Caja Madrid** exhibit hall (Tue–Sat 10:00–20:00, closed Mon, tel. 913-792-050, www.fundacioncajamadrid.es), across from the Descalzas Royal Monastery on Plaza San Martín.

Afterwards, if you're heading to Centro de Arte Reina Sofía and you're tired, hail a cab at the gate to zip straight there.

▲▲▲Centro de Arte Reina Sofía

Perhaps Europe's most enjoyable modern art museum, the Reina Sofía shows off an exceptional collection of 20th-century art in

what was Madrid's first public hospital (notice the iron-barred windows—facing the courtyard—for the mentally ill ward).

The new curator, who has a passion for cinema, has paired paintings with films from each decade throughout the museum. This provides a fascinating insight into the social context that inspired the art of Spain's tumultuous 20th century. Make a point to understand why a particular film was chosen, in order to gain an insight into Spain's 20th-century scars.

Cost and Hours: €6, free Sat afternoon after 14:30 (less crowded after 15:00) and all day Sun, always free to those under 18 and over 65. Even if admission is free when you visit, grab a ticket anyway. The museum is open Mon and Wed–Sat 10:00–21:00, Sun 10:00–14:30, closed Tue.

Location: It's across from the Atocha Metro station at Santa Isabel 52. In the Metro station, follow signs for Reina Sofía. At the opening into a square, look for the exterior glass elevators. There are two entrances: the old entrance (leads to permanent collection first; on Calle Sánchez Bustillo, on a big square close to the Metro stop) and the new entrance (mostly for tour groups).

Services and Information: Good brochure, no tours in English, hardworking €4 audioguide, no photos, free baggage storage. The *librería* just outside the new addition has a larger selection of Picasso and Surrealist reproductions than the main gift shop at the entrance. Tel. 914-675-062, www.museoreinasofia.es.

Touring the Museum: The permanent collection is on the second and fourth floors; temporary exhibits are on the first and third floors. Ride the fancy glass elevator to the second floor and follow the room numbers for art chronologically displayed from 1900 to 1940. The fourth floor continues the collection, from 1940 to 1980.

Picasso's *Guernica*: The museum is most famous for Pablo Picasso's *Guernica* (second floor, Room 7), an epic painting showing the horror of modern war. Notice the two rooms of studies Picasso did for *Guernica,* filled with iron-nail tears and screaming mouths. *Guernica* was displayed at the Museum of Modern Art in New York City until Franco's death, and now it reigns as Spain's national piece of art (see the sidebar on the next page spread).

Guernica

Perhaps the single most impressive piece of art in Spain is Pablo Picasso's *Guernica*. The monumental canvas—one of Europe's must-see sights—is not only a piece of art but a piece of history, capturing the horror of modern war in a modern style.

Pablo Picasso (1881–1973), a Spaniard, was in Paris in 1937, preparing an exhibition of paintings for the city's world's fair. Meanwhile, a bloody Civil War was being fought in his own country. The legally elected democratic government was being challenged by traditionalist right-wing forces under Francisco Franco. Franco would eventually win and rule the country with an iron fist for three decades.

On April 27, 1937, Guernica—a proud Basque market town in northern Spain—was the target of the world's first saturation-bombing raid on civilians. Franco gave permission to his fascist ally, Hitler, to use the town as a guinea pig to try out Germany's new air force. The raid leveled the town, causing destruction that was unheard-of at the time (though by 1944 it would be commonplace).

News of the bombing reached Picasso in Paris. He scrapped earlier plans and immediately set to work sketching scenes of the destruction as he imagined it. In a matter of weeks, he put these bomb-shattered shards together into a large mural (286 square feet). For the first time, the world could see the destructive force of the rising fascist movement—a prelude to World War II.

The bombs are falling, shattering the quiet village. A woman looks up at the sky (far right), horses scream (center), and a man falls from a horse and dies, while a wounded woman drags herself through the streets. She tries to escape, but her leg is too thick, dragging her down, like trying to run from something in a nightmare. On the left, a bull—a symbol of Spain—ponders it all, watching over a mother and her dead baby...a modern *pietà*. A woman in the center sticks her head out to see what's going on. The whole scene is lit from above by the stark light of a bare bulb. Picasso's painting threw a light on the brutality of Hitler and Franco, and suddenly the whole world was watching.

Picasso's abstract, Cubist style reinforces the message. It's as if he'd picked up the shattered shards and pasted them onto a canvas. The black and white tones are as gritty as the black-and-white newspaper photos that reported the bombing. The drab colors create a depressing, almost nauseating mood.

Picasso chose images with universal symbolism, making the work a commentary on all wars. Picasso himself said that the central horse, with the spear in its back, symbolizes humanity succumbing to brute force. The fallen rider's arm is severed and his sword is broken, more symbols of defeat. The bull, normally a proud symbol of strength and independence, is impotent and frightened. Near the bull, the dove of peace can do nothing but cry.

The bombing of Guernica—like the entire Spanish Civil War (1936-1939)—was an exercise in brutality. As one side captured a town, it might systematically round up every man, old and young—including priests—line them up, and shoot them in revenge for atrocities by the other side.

Thousands of people attended the Paris fair, and *Guernica* caused an immediate sensation. They could see the horror of modern war technology, the vain struggle of the Spanish Republicans, and the cold indifference of the fascist war machine. After the Paris exhibition, *Guernica* was exiled to America until Franco's death. Picasso also vowed never to return to Spain while Franco ruled. (Franco outlived him.)

With each passing year, the canvas seemed more and more prophetic—honoring not just the hundreds or thousands that died in Guernica, but also the 600,000 victims of Spain's bitter Civil War, and the 80 million worldwide that perished in World War II. Picasso put a human face on what we now call "collateral damage."

After pondering the destruction of war, visit the room farthest back from the painting (confusingly, also numbered 7) to see photos of Picasso creating this masterpiece.

The film in the room directly opposite *Guernica* is *España 1936*, produced by the Madrid government (Spain's "last red city") late in the war, with a fierce anti-Franco perspective. Of course, Franco won. The theater about 90 feet to the right of *Guernica* shows a 1971 satirical documentary that uses clips from post-civil war propaganda films praising Franco. It's called *Songs After a War* (*Canciones para después de una Guerra)* and couldn't be shown in Spain until after Franco's death.

Don't miss the model of the Spanish Pavilion at the 1937 Paris Expo. Picasso was readying to paint something light and "typically Spanish," such as flamenco and matadors, for the Expo. But the bombing of Guernica jolted him into the realization that "the real Spain" was a country torn by civil war. The pavilion was a vessel for anti-Franco propaganda and its centerpiece was *Guernica.*

After a 44-year exile in New York, *Guernica* finally came home to Spain on September 11, 1981.

Salvador Dalí: The museum houses an easy-to-enjoy collection by other modern artists, including more of Picasso and a mind-bending room of works by Salvador Dalí. The early Dalí is in Room 3; the signature Dalí works are in Room 12. *The Great Masturbator* is exhausting psychologically, depicting in its surrealism a lonely, highly sexual genius, in love with his muse, Gala, while she is still married to a French poet. Check out the propaganda movie produced by the Spanish Republic (pre-Franco) that shows the sad state of its people.

Room 10 is a treat for movie and Surrealism buffs: Two circa-1930 films—*The Andalusian Dog* and *The Golden Age*—by director Luis Buñuel, who had help from friends Dalí and the poet Federico García Lorca, play continuously. Lorca and Dalí were members of "The Generation of '27," a group of nonconformist creative Spanish bohemians who had a huge influence culturally and artistically on their era.

Near the Prado

▲**Retiro Park (Parque del Buen Retiro**)—Once the private domain of royalty, this majestic park has been a favorite of Madrid's commoners since Charles III decided to share it with his subjects in the late 18th century. Siesta in this 300-acre green-and-breezy escape from the city. At midday on Saturday and Sunday, the area around the lake becomes a street carnival, with jugglers, puppeteers, and lots of local color. These peaceful gardens offer great picnicking and people-watching. From the Retiro Metro stop, walk to the big lake (El Estanque), where you can cheaply rent a rowboat. Past the lake, a grand boulevard of statues leads to the Prado.

▲**Royal Botanical Garden (Real Jardín Botánico)**—After your Prado visit, you can take a lush and fragrant break in this sculpted park. Wander among trees from around the world. The flier in English explains that this is actually more than a park—it's a museum of plants (€2, daily 10:00–21:00, until 18:00 in winter, entry opposite Prado's Murillo/south entry, Plaza de Murillo 2).

▲**Naval Museum (Museo Naval)**—This museum tells the story of Spain's navy, from the Armada to today, in a plush and fascinating-to-boat-lovers exhibit. Given Spain's importance in maritime history, there's quite a story to tell (free, no English anywhere, Tue–Sun 10:00–14:00, closed Mon and Aug, a block north of the Prado across boulevard from Thyssen-Bornemisza Museum, Paseo del Prado 5, tel. 915-239-884, www.museonavalmadrid .com). Because this is a military facility, you'll need to show your passport to get in.

CaixaForum—Across the street from the Prado and Royal Botanical Garden, you'll find this impressive exhibit hall with sleek architecture and an outdoor hanging garden—a bushy wall festooned with greens designed by a French landscape artist. The forum, funded by La Caixa Bank, features world-class art exhibits—generally 20th-century art, well-described in English and changing three times a year. Ride the elevator to the top, where you'll find a chic café with €12 lunch specials and sperm-like lamps swarming down from the ceiling, and explore your way down (free, daily 10:00–20:00, Paseo del Prado 36, tel. 913-307-300, www.obrasocial.lacaixa.es).

Elsewhere in Madrid

Descalzas Royal Monastery (Monasterio de las Descalzas Reales)—Madrid's most visit-worthy monastery was founded in the 16th century by Philip II's sister, Joan of Habsburg (known to Spaniards as Juana, and to Austrians as Joanna). She's buried here. The monastery's chapels are decorated with fine art, Rubens-designed tapestries, and the heirlooms of the wealthy women who joined the order (the nuns were required to give a dowry). Because this is still a working Franciscan monastery, tourists can visit only when the nuns vacate the cloister, and the number of daily visitors is limited. The scheduled tours often sell out—come in the morning to buy your ticket, even if you want an afternoon tour (€5, visits guided in Spanish or English depending on demand, Tue–Thu and Sat 10:30–12:30 & 16:00–17:30, Fri 10:30–12:30, Sun 11:00–13:30, closed Mon, Plaza de las Descalzas Reales 3, near the Ópera Metro stop and just a short walk from Puerta del Sol, tel. 914-548-800). The free **Caja Madrid** exhibit hall is across the street from the monastery (Tue–Sat 10:00–20:00, closed Mon).

▲National Archaeological Museum (Museo Arqueológico Nacional)—This fine museum gives you a chronological walk through the story of Iberia on one convenient floor. With a rich collection of artifacts (but a maddening refusal to describe anything in English), it shows off the wonders of each age: Celtic pre-Roman, Roman, a fine and rare Visigothic section, Moorish, Romanesque, and beyond (always free; open Tue–Sat 9:30–20:00, Sun 9:30–15:00, closed Mon; Calle Serrano 13, Metro: Serrano or Colón, tel. 915-777-912). Outside, underground in the museum's garden, is an underwhelming replica artwork from northern Spain's Altamira Caves (big on bison), giving you a faded peek at the skill of the cave artists who created the originals 14,000 years ago.

Sorolla Museum (Museo Sorolla)—Joaquín Sorolla (1863–1923) is known for his portraits, landscapes, and use of light. It's a relaxing experience to stroll through the rooms of his former house and studio, especially to see the lazy beach scenes of his hometown Valencia. Take a break after your visit to reflect in the small garden in front of his house (€3, free on Sun, open Tue–Sat 9:30–20:00, Sun 10:00–15:00, closed Mon, General Martínez Campos 37, Metro: Iglesia, tel. 913-101-584, http://museosorolla.mcu.es).

Municipal Museum (Museo Municipal)—Follow the history of Madrid in old paintings and models (but no English). As you enter, notice Pedro de Ribera's fine Baroque door featuring "St. James the Moor-Slayer." The museum is closed for a major renovation through 2011 (Calle Fuencarral 78, Metro: Tribunal or Bilbao, tel. 917-011-863).

▲Clothing Museum (Museo del Traje)—This museum shows the history of clothing from the 18th century until today. In a cool and air-conditioned chronological sweep, the museum's one floor of exhibits includes regional ethnic costumes, a look at how bullfighting and the French influenced styles, accessories through the ages, and Spanish flappers. The only downside of this marvelous modern museum is that it's a long way from anything else of interest (€3, free Sat 14:30–19:00 and all day Sun, open Tue–Sat 9:30–19:00, Sun 10:00–15:00, closed Mon, last entry 30 min before closing, Avenida Juan Herrera 2; Metro: Moncloa and a longish walk, bus #46, or taxi; tel. 915-497-150).

▲Chapel of San Antonio de la Florida—In this simple little Neoclassical chapel from the 1790s, Francisco de Goya's tomb stares up at a splendid cupola filled with his own proto-Impressionist frescoes. He frescoed this using the same unique technique that he used for his "dark paintings." Use the mirrors to enjoy the drama and energy he infused into this marvelously restored masterpiece (free, Tue–Fri 9:30–20:00, Sat–Sun 10:00–14:00, closed Mon,

Glorieta de San Antonio de la Florida, tel. 915-420-722). This chapel is a five-minute walk down Paseo de San Antonio de la Florida from Metro: Príncipe Pío (and its bus station, serving Segovia).

Royal Tapestry Factory (Real Fábrica de Tapices)—Have a look at traditional tapestry-making (€3.50, by tour only, on the half-hour, Mon–Fri 10:00–14:00, closed Sat–Sun and Aug, some English tours, Calle Fuenterrabia 2, Metro: Menendez Pelayo, take Gutenberg exit, tel. 914-340-550). You can actually order a tailor-made tapestry (starting at $10,000).

Temple de Debod—In 1968, Egypt gave Spain its own ancient temple. It was a gift of the Egyptian government, which was grateful for Franco's help in rescuing monuments that had been threatened by the rising Nile waters above the Aswan Dam. Consequently, Madrid is the only place I can think of in Europe where you can actually wander through an intact original Egyptian temple—complete with fine carved reliefs from 200 B.C. (free; April–Sept Tue–Fri 10:00–14:00 & 18:00–20:00, Sat–Sun 10:00–14:00, closed Mon; Oct–March Tue–Fri 9:45–13:45 & 16:15–18:15, Sat–Sun 10:00–14:00, closed Mon, in Parque de Montaña, north of the Royal Palace). Set in a romantic park that locals love for its great city views (especially at sunset), the temple—as well as its art—is well-described. Popular as the view may be, the uninspiring "grand Madrid view" only causes me to wonder why anyone would build a city here.

Experiences in Madrid

▲▲**Self-Guided Bus Tour: Paseo de la Castellana**—Tourists risk leaving Madrid without ever seeing the modern "Manhattan" side of town. But it's easy to do. From the Prado Museum, bus #27 makes the trip straight north along Paseo del Prado and then Paseo de la Castellana, through the no-nonsense skyscraper part of this city of more than three million. The line ends at what's called Puerta de Europa (Gate of Europe), twin office towers that are designed to lean at a 15-degree angle. This trip is simple and cheap (€1, buses run every 10 min, sit on the right if possible, beware of pickpockets). You just joyride for 30 minutes to the last stop, get out when everyone else does, ogle the skyscrapers, and catch the Metro for a 20-minute ride back to the city's center. At twilight, when fountains and facades are floodlit, the ride is particularly enjoyable.

Bus #27 rumbles from Atocha Station past the Royal Botanical Garden (opposite McDonald's) and the Velázquez entrance to the Prado (if you're starting from here, catch the bus from the museum side to head north).

Look out for these landmarks: the Prado Museum (right); a square with a fountain of Neptune (left); an obelisk and war memorial to those who have died for Spain (right, with the stock market behind it); the Naval Museum (right); Plaza de Cibeles with the fancy post office (right, now used as City Hall; other huge buildings such as the Bank of Spain line the square); and then the National Library (right).

When you come to a square with a statue of Columbus, it marks the end of the historic town and the beginning of the modern city. At this point the boulevard changes its name. It used to be named for Franco; now it's named for the people he no longer rules—*la Castellana* (Castilians). Next comes the American Embassy (hard to see behind its fortified wall, right) and Franco's ministries (left, typical fascist architecture, c. 1940s, some still used). Continuing up the boulevard, look left to see the Picasso Tower (which looks like one of New York's former World Trade Center towers, because both buildings were designed by the same architect), the huge Bernabéu soccer stadium (right, home of Real Madrid, Europe's most successful soccer team), and the Ministry of Defense (left).

Your trip ends at Plaza de Castilla, where you can't miss the avant-garde Puerta de Europa, consisting of twin leaning office towers, one with the big green logo of the Bank of Madrid. In the distance, you can see three of the tallest buildings in Spain. The plaza sports a futuristic obelisk by contemporary Spanish architect Santiago Calatrava.

It's the end of the line for the bus and for you. There is an easy, direct return to Puerta del Sol via the Metro, or cross the street and ride bus #27 along the same route back to the Prado or Atocha Station.

▲**Electric Minibus Joyride Through Lavapiés**—For a relaxing ride through the characteristic old center of Madrid, hop little electric minibus #M1 (€1, 5/hr, 20-min trip, 8:00–20:00). These are designed mostly for local seniors who could use a lift (offer your seat if there's a senior standing). Catch the minibus at the Sevilla Metro stop and simply ride it to the end (Metro: Embajadores). Enjoy this gritty slice of workaday Madrid—both people and architecture—as you roll slowly through Plaza Santa Ana, down a bit of the pedestrianized Calle de las Huertas, past newly gentrified Tirso de Molina (with junkies now replaced by a family-friendly flower market), through Plaza de Lavapiés and a barrio of African and Bangladeshi immigrants until you get to Embajadores. From there you can catch the next #M1 minibus (which returns to the Sevilla Metro stop along a different route) or descend into the subway system.

▲▲**Bullfight**—Madrid's Plaza de Toros hosts Spain's top bullfights on some Sundays and holidays from March through mid-October, and nearly every day during the San Isidro festival (May through early June—often sold out long in advance). Fights start between 17:00 and 21:00 (early in spring and fall, late in summer). The bullring is at the Ventas Metro stop (a 15-min Metro ride from Puerta del Sol, tel. 913-562-200, www.las-ventas.com).

MADRID

Bullfight tickets range from €5 to €150. There are no bad seats at the Plaza de Toros; paying more gets you in the shade and/or closer to the gore. (The action often intentionally occurs in the shade to reward the expensive-ticket holders.) To be close to the bullring, choose areas 8, 9, or 10; for shade: 1, 2, 9, or 10; for shade/sun: 3 or 8; for the sun and cheapest seats: 4, 5, 6, or 7. Note these key words: *corrida*—a real fight with professionals; *novillada*—rookie matadors and younger bulls. Getting tickets through your hotel or a booking office is convenient, but they add 20 percent or more and don't sell the cheap seats. There are two booking offices; call both before you buy: at Plaza del Carmen 1 (Mon–Sat 9:30–13:00 & 16:30–19:00, Sun 9:30–13:30, tel. 915-319-131, or buy online at www.bullfightticketsmadrid.com; run by English-speaking José, who also sells soccer tickets) and at Calle Victoria 3 (Mon–Fri 10:00–14:00 & 17:00–19:00, Sat–Sun 10:00–14:00, tel. 915-211-213). To save money, you can stand in the ticket line at the bullring. Except for important bullfights—or during the San Isidro festival—there are generally plenty of seats available. About a thousand tickets are held back to be sold in the five days leading up to a fight, including the day of the fight. Scalpers hang out before the popular fights at the Calle Victoria booking office. Beware: Those buying scalped tickets are breaking the law and can lose the ticket with no recourse.

For a dose of the experience, you can buy a cheap ticket and just stay to see a couple of bullfights. Each fight takes about 20 minutes, and the event consists of six bulls over two hours. Or, to keep your distance but get a sense of the ritual and gore, tour the bull bar on Plaza Mayor (described earlier as part of the city walk).

Madrid's **Bullfighting Museum** (Museo Taurino) is not as good as Sevilla's or Ronda's (free, Tue–Fri 9:30–14:30, Sun 10:00–13:00, closed Sat and Mon and early on fight days, at the back of bullring, tel. 917-251-857).

MADRID

"Football" and Bernabéu Stadium—Madrid, like most of Europe, is enthusiastic about soccer (which they call *fútbol*). The Real Madrid team plays to a spirited local crowd Saturdays and Sundays from September through May (tickets from €50—sold at bullfight box offices listed above). One of the most popular sightseeing activities among European visitors to Madrid is touring the 80,000-seat stadium. The €15 tour includes the box seats, dressing rooms, technical zone, playing field, trophy room, and a big panoramic stadium view (daily 10:00–19:00, Metro: Santiago Bernabéu, www.realmadrid.com, tel. 913-984-300).

Shopping in Madrid

Shoppers focus on the colorful pedestrian area between Gran Vía and Puerta del Sol. The giant Spanish department store El Corte Inglés, a block off Puerta del Sol, is a handy place to pick up just about anything you need (Mon–Sat 10:00–22:00, Sun 11:00–21:00).

El Rastro: Europe's biggest flea market, rated ▲, is a field day for shoppers, people-watchers, and thieves (Sundays only, 9:00–15:00, best before 11:00). Thousands of stalls titillate more than a million browsers with mostly new junk. Locals have lamented the tackiness of El Rastro lately—you'll find cheap underwear and bootleg CDs, but no real treasures. Start at the Plaza Mayor, with its stamp- and coin-collectors market (see below),

and head south or take the Metro to Tirso de Molina. Walk downhill, finishing at the Puerta de Toledo Metro stop. El Rastro offers a fascinating chance to see gangs of young thieves overwhelming and ripping off naive tourists with no police anywhere in sight. Seriously: Don't even bring a wallet. The pickpocket action is brutal, and tourists are targeted.

While the flea market can be a downer, Europe's biggest stamp and coin market, thriving simultaneously on Plaza Mayor, is a genteel delight. Watch the old-timers paging lovingly through each other's albums, looking for win-win trades.

Fans: Casa de Diego sells *abanicos* (fans), *mantones* (typical Spanish shawls), *castañuelas* (castanets), *peinetas* (hair combs), and umbrellas. Even if you're not in the market, it's fun to watch the women flip open their final fan choices before buying (Mon–Sat 9:30–20:00, closed Sun, Puerta del Sol 12, tel. 915-226-643).

Classical Guitars: Guitar-lovers know that the world's finest classical guitars are made in Spain. Several of the top workshops, within an easy walk of Puerta del Sol, offer inviting little show-rooms with a peek at their craft and an opportunity to strum the final product. Consider the workshops of José Romero (Calle de Espoz y Mina 30, tel. 915-214-218) and José Ramirez (Calle de la Paz 8, tel. 915-314-229). Union Musical is a popular guitar shop off Puerta del Sol (Carrera de San Jerónimo 26, tel. 914-293-877). If you're shopping, be prepared to spend €1,000.

Nightlife in Madrid

Those into clubbing may have to wait until after midnight for the most popular places to even open, much less start hopping. Spain has a reputation for partying very late, not ending until offices open in the morning. If you're people-watching early in the morning, it's actually hard to know who is finishing their day and who's just starting it. Even if you're not a party animal after midnight, make a point to be out with the happy masses, luxuriating in the cool evening air between 22:00 and midnight. The scene is absolutely unforgettable.

▲▲▲Paseo—Just walking the streets of Madrid seems to be the way the Madrileños spend their evenings. Even past midnight on a hot summer night, entire families with little kids are strolling, enjoying tiny beers and tapas in a series of bars, licking ice cream, and greeting their neighbors. A good area to wander is along Gran Vía (from about Metro: Callao to Plaza de España). Or start at Puerta del Sol, and explore in the direction of Plaza Santa Ana. The newly pedestrianized Calle de las Huertas is also understand-ably popular with strollers.

▲Zarzuela—For a delightful look at Spanish light opera that even English-speakers can enjoy, try zarzuela. Guitar-strumming Napoleons in red capes; buxom women with masks, fans, and castanets; Spanish-speaking pharaohs; melodramatic spotlights; and aficionados clapping and singing along from the cheap seats, where the acoustics are best—this is zarzuela...the people's opera. Originating in Madrid, zarzuela is known for its satiric humor and surprisingly good music. You can buy tickets at Theater Zarzuela, which alternates between zarzuela, ballet, and opera throughout the year (€16–40, box office open 12:00–18:00 for advance tickets or until showtime for that day, Jovellanos 4, near the Prado, Metro: Sevilla or Banco de España, tel. 915-245-400, http://teatrodela zarzuela.mcu.es; to purchase online, go to the theater section of www.servicaixa.com and choose the English version). The TI's monthly guide has a special zarzuela listing.

▲▲Flamenco—Although Sevilla is the capital of flamenco, Madrid has three easy and affordable options. And on summer evenings, Madrid puts on live flamenco events in the Royal Palace gardens (ask TI for details).

Taberna Casa Patas attracts big-name flamenco artists. You'll quickly understand why this intimate (30 tables, 120 seats) and smoky venue is named "House of Feet." Since this is for locals as well as tour groups, the flamenco is contemporary and may be jazzier than your notion—it depends on who's performing (€31, Mon–Thu at 22:30, Fri–Sat at 21:00 and 24:00, closed Sun, 75–90 min, price includes cover and first drink, reservations smart, no flash cameras, Cañizares 10, tel. 913-690-496, www.casapatas .com). Its restaurant is a logical spot for dinner before the show (€30 dinners, Mon–Sat from 20:00). Or, since it's three blocks south of the recommended Plaza Santa Ana tapas bars, this could be your post-tapas-crawl entertainment.

Las Carboneras, more downscale, is an easygoing, folksy little place a few steps from Plaza Mayor with a nightly hour-long flamenco show (€33 includes an entry and a drink, €61 gets you a table up front with dinner and unlimited cheap drinks if you reserve ahead, manager Enrique promises a €5 per person discount if you book direct and show this book in 2010, Mon–Thu at 22:30 and often at 20:30, Fri–Sat at 20:30 and 23:00, closed Sun, reservations recommended, Plaza del Conde de Miranda 1, tel. 915-428-677). While Las Carboneras lacks the pretense of Casa Patas, Casa Patas has better-quality artists and a riveting seriousness. Considering that Las Carboneras raised its prices to essentially match Casa Patas, the "House of Feet" is the better value.

Las Tablas Flamenco offers a less expensive nightly show respecting the traditional art of flamenco. You'll sit in a plain room with a mix of tourists and locals in a modern, nondescript office block just over the freeway from Plaza de España (€24 with drink, reasonable drink prices, Sun–Thu 22:30, Fri–Sat 20:00 & 22:00, 75-min show, corner of Calle de Ferraz and Cuesta de San Vicente, tel. 915-420-520, www.lastablasmadrid.com).

Regardless of what your hotel receptionist may want to sell you, other flamenco places—such as Arco de Cuchilleros (Calle de los Cuchilleros 7), Café de Chinitas (Calle Torija 7, just off Plaza Mayor), Corral de la Morería (Calle de Morería 17), and Torres Bermejas (off Gran Vía)—are filled with tourists and pushy waiters.

Mesones—These long, skinny cave-like bars, famous for customers drinking and singing late into the night, line the lane called Cava de San Miguel, just west of Plaza Mayor. If you were to toss lowbrow locals, Spanish karaoke, electric keyboards, crass tourists, cheap sangria, and greasy calamari into a late-night blender and turn it on, this is what you'd get. It's generally lively only on Friday and Saturday.

Late-Night and Jazz Bars—If you're just picking up speed at midnight, and looking for a place filled with old tiles and a Gen-X crowd, power into **Bar Viva Madrid** (daily 13:00–3:00 in the morning, downhill from Plaza Santa Ana on Calle Manuel Fernández y González, tel. 914-293-640). The same street has other late-night bars filled with music. Or hike on over to **Chocolatería San Ginés** for a dessert of *churros con chocolate*.

For live jazz, **Café Central** is the old town favorite. Since 1982, it's been known as the place where rising stars get their start (€14, 22:00 nightly, cheap drinks, great scene, Plaza del Angel 10, tel. 913-694-143, www.cafecentralmadrid.com).

Movies—During Franco's days, movies were always dubbed into Spanish. As a result, movies in Spain remain about the most often dubbed in Europe. Dubbing was encouraged by Franco's xenophobia and the need to censor popular entertainment during his rule. When dubbing a movie, you can change the meaning and almost no one knows. To see a movie with its original soundtrack, look for *"V.O."* (meaning "original version"). Cine Ideal, with nine screens, is a good place for the latest films in *V.O.* (€7.50, 5-min walk south of Puerta del Sol at Calle del Dr. Cortezo 6, tel. 913-692-518 for info). For extensive listings, see the *Guía del Ocio* entertainment guide (€1 at newsstands, www.guiadelocio.com) or a local newspaper.

Sleeping in Madrid

Madrid has plenty of centrally located budget hotels and *pensiónes*. Most of the accommodations I've listed are within a few minutes' walk of Puerta del Sol.

You'll have no trouble finding a sleepable double for €40, a good double for €80, and a modern, air-conditioned double with

Sleep Code

(€1 = about $1.40, country code: 34)
S = Single, **D** = Double/Twin, **T** = Triple, **Q** = Quad, **b** = bathroom, **s** = shower only. Unless otherwise noted, credit cards are accepted, English is spoken, and breakfast is *not* included.

To help you easily sort through these listings, I've divided the rooms into three categories, based on the price for a standard double room with bath during high season:

$$$ Higher Priced—Most rooms €100 or more.
  $$ Moderately Priced—Most rooms between €70–100.
    $ Lower Priced—Most rooms €70 or less.

all the comforts for €110. Prices vary throughout the year at bigger hotels, but remain about the same for the smaller hotels and *hostales*. It's almost always easy to find a place. Anticipate full hotels only during May (the San Isidro festival, celebrating Madrid's patron saint with bullfights and zarzuelas—especially around his feast day on May 15) and September (when conventions can clog the city). During the hot months of July and August, prices can be soft—always ask for a discount.

Given the current financial downturn, big hotels are coming up empty and are desperately discounting, which is taking lots of business away from smaller hotels that are already inexpensive. To get the best price, email big business-class hotels and let them bid for your business.

With all of Madrid's street noise, I'd request the highest floor possible. Also, twin-bedded rooms are generally a bit larger than double-bedded rooms for the same price. During slow times, drop-ins can often score a room in business-class hotels for just a few euros more than the budget hotels (which don't have prices that fluctuate as wildly with demand).

Fancier Places in the Pedestrian Zone Between Puerta del Sol and Gran Vía

These business-class hotels are good values for those wanting to spend a little more. Their formal prices may be inflated, but most offer weekend and summer discounts when it's slow. Again, if you're interested in staying at a business-class hotel, email around for the best price. Drivers pay about €24 a day in garages. Use Metro: Sol for all but Hotel Opera (Metro: Ópera).

$$$ Hotel Liabeny rents 220 plush, spacious, business-class rooms offering all the comforts (Sb-€110, Db-€125, Tb-€176, 10 percent cheaper mid-July–Aug and Fri–Sat, breakfast-€16, air-con, sauna, gym, off Plaza del Carmen at Salud 3, tel. 915-319-000, fax 915-327-421, www.liabeny.es, info@liabeny.es).

$$$ Hotel Preciados, a four-star business hotel, has 73 fine, sleek, and modern rooms as well as elegant lounges. It's well-located and reasonably priced for the luxury it provides (Db-€125-160, prices are often soft, checking Web specials in advance or drop-ping in will likely snag a room for around €100, breakfast-€15, just off Plaza de Santo Domingo at Calle Preciados 37, tel. 914-544-400, fax 914-544-401, www.preciadoshotel.com, preciadoshotel @preciadoshotel.com).

$$$ Hotel Carlos V is a Best Western with 67 sharp high-ceilinged rooms, elegant breakfast, and a pleasant lounge (Sb-€95, standard Db-€115, Tb-€135, tax not included, breakfast-€9, air-con, non-smoking floors, elevator, Wi-Fi, Maestro Victoria 5,

Madrid's Center—Hotels and Restaurants

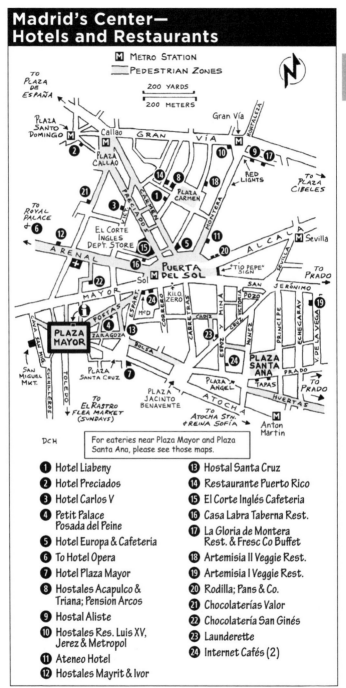

- METRO STATION
- PEDESTRIAN ZONES

200 YARDS
200 METERS

For eateries near Plaza Mayor and Plaza Santa Ana, please see those maps.

DCH

1 Hotel Liabeny
2 Hotel Preciados
3 Hotel Carlos V
4 Petit Palace Posada del Peine
5 Hotel Europa & Cafeteria
6 To Hotel Opera
7 Hotel Plaza Mayor
8 Hostales Acapulco & Triana; Pension Arcos
9 Hostal Aliste
10 Hostales Res. Luis XV, Jerez & Metropol
11 Ateneo Hotel
12 Hostales Mayrit & Ivor

13 Hostal Santa Cruz
14 Restaurante Puerto Rico
15 El Corte Inglés Cafeteria
16 Casa Labra Taberna Rest.
17 La Gloria de Montera Rest. & Fresc Co Buffet
18 Artemisia II Veggie Rest.
19 Artemisia I Veggie Rest.
20 Rodilla; Pans & Co.
21 Chocolaterías Valor
22 Chocolatería San Ginés
23 Launderette
24 Internet Cafés (2)

tel. 915-314-100, fax 915-313-761, www.hotelcarlosv.com, recepcion @hotelcarlosv.com).

$$$ Petit Palace Posada del Peine feels like part of a big modern chain (which it is), but fills its well-located old building with fresh, efficient character. Behind the ornate and sparkling Old World facade is a comfortable and modern business-class hotel with 67 rooms just a block from Plaza Mayor (Db-€100–160 depending on demand, tax not included, breakfast-€9, air-con, Calle Postas 17, tel. 915-238-151, fax 915-232-993, www.hthoteles .com, pos@hthoteles.com).

$$ Hotel Europa, with sleek marble, red carpet runners along the halls, happy Muzak charm, and an attentive staff, is a tremendous value. It rents 103 squeaky-clean rooms, many with balconies overlooking the pedestrian zone or an inner courtyard. They are honest and offer a straight price (Sb-€74, Db-€92, Db with view-€110, Tb-€130, Qb-€155, Quint/b-€175, tax not included, breakfast extra, air-con, elevator, free Internet access, Calle del Carmen 4, tel. 915-212-900, fax 915-214-696, www.hoteleuropa.net, info @hoteleuropa.net, run by Antonio and Fernando Garaban and their helpful and jovial staff, Javi and Jim). The convenient Europa cafeteria-restaurant next door is a lively and convivial scene—fun for breakfast.

$$ Hotel Ópera, a serious and contemporary hotel with 79 classy rooms, is located just off Plaza Isabel II, a four-block walk from Puerta del Sol toward the Royal Palace (Db-€75–95 but prices spike wildly with demand, includes breakfast, air-con, elevator, free Internet access, ask for a higher floor—there are nine—to avoid street noise, Cuesta de Santo Domingo 2, Metro: Ópera, tel. 915-412-800, fax 915-416-923, www.hotelopera.com, reservas @hotelopera.com). Hotel Ópera's cafeteria is understandably popular. Consider their "singing dinners"—great operetta music with a delightful dinner—offered nightly at 22:00 (around €65, reservations smart, call 915-426-382 or reserve at hotel).

$$ Hotel Plaza Mayor, with 34 solidly outfitted rooms, is tastefully decorated and beautifully situated a block off Plaza Mayor (Sb-€65, Db-€85, superior Db-€95, Tb-€115, director Leo offers travelers who book direct with this book a free breakfast in 2010, air-con, elevator, Wi-Fi, Calle Atocha 2, tel. 913-600-606, fax 913-600-610, www.h-plazamayor.com, info@h-plaza mayor.com).

Cheaper Bets near Puerta del Sol and Gran Vía

These three are all in the same building at Calle de la Salud 13, overlooking Plaza del Carmen—a little square with a sleepy, almost Parisian ambience.

$ Hostal Acapulco rents 16 bright rooms with air-condition-ing and all the big hotel gear. The neighborhood is quiet enough that it's smart to request a room with a balcony (Sb-€49–54, Db-€59–64, Tb-€77–80, elevator, free Internet access and Wi-Fi, fourth floor, tel. 915-311-945, fax 915-322-329, hostal_acapulco @yahoo.es, Ana and Marco).

$ Hostal Triana, also a fine deal, is bigger—with 40 rooms—and offers a little less charm for a little less money (Sb-€42, Db-€55, Tb-€75, includes taxes, rooms facing the square have air-con and cost €3 extra, other rooms have fans, elevator, free Wi-Fi, first floor, tel. 915-326-812, fax 915-229-729, www.hostaltriana .com, triana@hostaltriana.com, Víctor González).

$ Pension Arcos is tiny, granny-run, and old-fashioned—it's been in the Hernández family since 1936. You can reserve by phone—in Spanish, and you must pay in cash. But its five rooms are clean, quiet, and served by an elevator. You also have access to a tiny roof terrace and a nice little lounge. For cheap beds in a great locale, assuming you can communicate, this place is unbeatable (D-€36, Db-€40, fifth floor, air-con, closed Aug, tel. 915-324-994, Anuncia and Sabino).

More Cheap Sleeps at the Top of Calle de la Montera

These three places are a few minutes' walk from Puerta del Sol and a stone's throw from Gran Vía at the top of Calle de la Montera, which some dislike because of the young prostitutes that hang out here. They're legal, and the zone is otherwise safe and comfortable.

$ Hostal Aliste rents 11 decent rooms in a dreary-yet-secure building at a great price for readers of this book (Sb-€30, Db-€40, extra bed-€20, air-con, elevator, Internet access, Caballero de Gracia 6, third floor, tel. 915-215-979, h.aliste@teleline.es, Rachael and Edward speak English).

$ Hostal Residencia Luis XV is a big, plain, well-run, and clean place offering a good value. It's on a quiet eighth floor (there's an elevator). It can be smoky. They also run the 36-room **Hostal Jerez**—similar in every way—on the sixth floor (Sb-€45, Db-€59, Tb-€75, includes tax, air-con, elevator, free Wi-Fi with this book in 2010, Calle de la Montera 47, tel. 915-221-021, fax 915-221-350, www.hrluisxv.net, reservas@hrluisxv.net).

$ Hostal Metropol is a big, colorful, and very youthful youth hostel with 130 beds and an inviting pub and lounge (bed-€18, 4–6 beds per room, always co-ed, Sb-€35, Db-€60, includes a fitted sheet and breakfast, towel not included, free Internet access, Calle de la Montera 47, first floor, tel. 915-212-935, fax 915-212-934, www.metropolhostel.com, hotel-metropol@terra.es).

MADRID

Other Budget Beds in the Center

$$ Ateneo Hotel, just steps off Puerta del Sol, lacks public spaces and character, but its 38 rooms are close to business-class (Db-€75–90, occasionally less or more, air-con, Internet access, Calle de la Montera 22, tel. 915-212-012, fax 915-233-136, www.hotel-ateneo.com, info@hotel-ateneo.com).

$ Hostal Mayrit rents 28 rooms with thoughtful touches on the newly pedestrianized Calle del Arenal (Sb-€50, Db-€65, air-con, near Metro: Ópera at Calle del Arenal 24, third floor, tel. 915-480-403). They also run **Hostal Ivor** downstairs (same comfort level and prices).

$ Hostal Santa Cruz, simple and well-located, has 16 rooms at a good price (Sb-€45, Db-€58, Tb-€85, air-con, a block off Plaza Mayor at Plaza de Santa Cruz 6, second floor, tel. 915-522-441, fax 915-237-088, www.hostalsantacruz.com, info@hostalsantacruz.com).

$ Madrid Municipal Youth Hostel (Albergue Juvenil Madrid) is the big new 132-bed hostel in town. It has four to six beds per room with lockers, modern bathrooms, and lots of extras such as bike rentals, billiards, and movies (dorm bed-about €22, co-ed rooms, Internet access, closed 11:00–15:00, Metro: Tribunal, then walk two minutes down Calle de Barceló to Calle de Mejia Lequerica 21, tel. 915-939-688, fax 915-939-684, www.ajmadrid.es, info@ajmadrid.es).

Near the Prado

To locate the following three places, please see "Madrid's Museum Neighborhood" map.

$$$ Hotel Lope de Vega offers good business-class hotel value near the Prado. It is a "cultural-themed" hotel inspired by the 17th-century writer Lope de Vega. With 60 rooms, it feels cozy and friendly for a formal hotel (Sb-€105, Db-€115–135, Tb-€180, one child sleeps free, prices about 20 percent lower Fri–Sun and during most of the summer, air-con, elevator, Internet access, parking-€23/day, Calle Lope de Vega 49, tel. 913-600-011, fax 914-292-391, www.hotellopedevega.com, lopedevega@hotellopedevega.com).

At Cervantes 34: Two fine budget *hostales* are at Cervantes 34 (Metro: Antón Martín—but not handy to Metro). Both are homey, with inviting lounge areas; neither serves breakfast. **$ Hostal Gonzalo** has 15 spotless, comfortable rooms on the third floor and is well-run by friendly and helpful Javier. It's deservedly in all the guidebooks, so reserve in advance (Sb-€45, Db-€55, Tb-€70, air-con, elevator, Wi-Fi, tel. 914-292-714, fax 914-202-007, www.hostalgonzalo.com, hostal@hostalgonzalo.com). Downstairs, the nearly as polished **$ Hostal Cervantes** also has 15 rooms (Sb-€50, Db-€60, Tb-€75, includes tax, cheaper when slow and for longer stays, some rooms with air-con, Internet access and Wi-Fi, tel. 914-298-365, fax 914-292-745, www.hostal-cervantes.com, correo @hostal-cervantes.com, Fabio).

Eating in Madrid

In Spain, only Barcelona rivals Madrid for taste-bud thrills. You have three dining choices: a memorable, atmospheric sit-down meal in a well-chosen restaurant; a forgettable, basic sit-down meal; or a stand-up meal of tapas in a bar...or four. Unless otherwise noted, these places start serving lunch at 13:00 or 13:30 and dinner from 20:30. You'll often find the places nearly empty with a few forlorn early-bird tourists and then thriving with locals after 14:00 and 22:00. Many restaurants close in August. Madrid has famously good tap water, and waiters willingly serve it free—just ask for *agua del grifo*.

I've grouped the recommended restaurants by neighborhood—near Plaza Mayor, Plaza Santa Ana, the Royal Palace, the Prado, and Puerta del Sol. I've listed a range of eateries, from splurges to cheap eats to fun pub crawls and churros with chocolate. Enjoy!

Near Plaza Mayor
Fine Dining
Restaurante Casa Paco is a Madrid tradition. Check out its old walls plastered with autographed photos of local celebrities who have enjoyed their signature dish—ox grilled over a coal fire. While popular with tourists, the place is authentic, confident, and uncompromising—let non-smokers be damned. It's a worthwhile splurge if you want to dine out well and carnivorously (€15–25 plates, ox sold by weight, 200 grams—which is almost half a pound—is a hearty steak, Plaza de la Puerta Cerrada 11, tel. 913-663-166).

Sobrino del Botín is a hit with many Americans because "Hemingway ate here." It's grotesquely touristy, pricey, and the last place Papa would go now...but still, people love it, and the food is excellent (roast suckling pig is the specialty). If phoning to make a reservation, choose the upstairs for a still-traditional, but airier style over the downstairs, which has a dark, medieval-cellar ambience (€30 meals, daily 13:00–16:00 & 20:00–24:00, a block downhill from Plaza Mayor at Cuchilleros 17, tel. 913-664-217).

Posada de la Villa serves Castilian cuisine in a 17th-century inn. This sprawling, multi-floor restaurant has open-beam ceilings, which give it a rustic flair. Peek into the big oven to see the baby pigs about to make some diner happy. If you're not going to Toledo or Sevilla, this is a good place to try roast lamb, the house specialty (€30 meals, closed Sun and Aug, Calle Cava Baja 9, tel. 913-661-860). Posada de la Villa's twin, **Taberna del Capitan Alatriste,** is

MADRID

Eating near Plaza Mayor

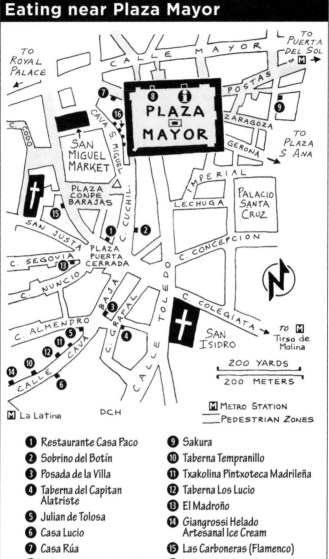

1 Restaurante Casa Paco
2 Sobrino del Botín
3 Posada de la Villa
4 Taberna del Capitan Alatriste
5 Julian de Tolosa
6 Casa Lucio
7 Casa Rúa
8 Torre del Oro Bar Andalú
9 Sakura
10 Taberna Tempranillo
11 Txakolina Pintxoteca Madrileña
12 Taberna Los Lucio
13 El Madroño
14 Giangrossi Helado Artesanal Ice Cream
15 Las Carboneras (Flamenco)
16 Mesones ("Cave Bars")

more fresh and modern, a half-block away, and run by the same owners. They serve classic cuisine with lots of game under open beams in a stylish medieval vault (€25 plates, closed Mon, Grafal 7, tel. 913-661-883).

Julian de Tolosa is chic, pricey, elegantly simple, and popular with natives who know good food. They offer a small, quality menu of Navarra's regional cuisine, from T-bone steak *(chuletón)* to red *tolosa* beans, in a spacious, sane setting with nothing touristic (€40 meals, closed Sun, Calle Cava Baja 18, tel. 913-658-210).

Casa Lucio is a favorite splurge among power-dressing Madrileños. The king and queen of Spain eat in this formal place, but it's accessible to commoners. This is a fine restaurant for a special night out and a full-blown meal, but you pay extra for this place's fame (€40 for dinner, nightly from 21:00, closed Aug, Calle Cava Baja 35; unless you're the king or queen, reserve several days in advance—and don't even bother on weekends; tel. 913-653-252).

Eating Cheaply

Madrileños enjoy a bite to eat on Plaza Mayor (without its high costs) by grabbing food to go from a nearby bar and just planting themselves somewhere on the square to eat (squid sandwiches are popular). But for many tourists, dinner at a sidewalk café right on Plaza Mayor is worth the premium price (consider Cervecería Pulpito, southwest corner of the square at #10).

Squid Sandwiches: Plaza Mayor is famous for its *bocadillos de calamares*. For a tasty €2.50 squid-ring sandwich, line up at **Casa Rúa** at Plaza Mayor's northwest corner, a few steps up Calle Ciudad Rodrigo (daily 9:00–23:00). Hanging up behind the bar is a photo-advertisement of Plaza Mayor from the 1950s, when the square contained a park.

Bullfighting Bar: The **Torre del Oro Bar Andalú** on Plaza  Mayor has walls lined with grisly bullfight photos. While this place is good for drinks, you pay a premium for the tapas and food… the cost of munching amidst all that bullephenalia while enjoying their excellent Plaza Mayor outdoor seating (daily 8:00–15:00 & 18:00–24:00).

Japanese Restaurant: **Sakura** is nothing special but offers a welcome, ham-free oasis with air-conditioning and a hot face towel. Japanese-run, it serves a good €10 lunch special (daily from 12:00 and from 19:30, Calle de San Cristóbal 11, tel. 915-321-089).

Tapas on Calle Cava Baja, South of Plaza Mayor

Just three minutes south of Plaza Mayor, Calle Cava Baja fills each evening with mostly young, professional locals prowling for chic tapas and social fun. Tapas are the toothpick appetizers, salads, and deep-fried foods traditionally served in Spanish bars. Come at night only and treat the entire street as a destination. I've listed a few standards, but excellent new eateries are always opening up. For a good, authentic Madrid dinner experience, take time to survey the many options along this street and then choose your favorites. Remember, it's easier and touristy early, jammed with locals later. (If you want a formal dining experience on this street, try Posada de la Villa Julian de Tolosa, or Casa Lucio, recommended in "Fine Dining," earlier). These Calle Cava Baja tapas bars are worth special consideration:

Taberna Tempranillo, ideal for hungry wine-lovers, offers fancy tapas and fine wine by the glass (see listing on the board). While there are a few tables, the bar is just right for hanging out. With a phrasebook in hand or a spirit of adventure, use their fascinating menu to assemble your dream meal. It's packed and full of commotion—the crowds can be overwhelming. Arrive by 20:00 or plan to wait (closed Aug, Calle Cava Baja 38, tel. 913-641-532).

Txakolina Pintxoteca Madrileña is a thriving bar serving Basque-style *pinchos* (tiny fancy sandwiches—*pintxo* in Basque) to a young crowd (€3/*pincho*, Calle Cava Baja 26, tel. 913-664-877).

Taberna Los Lucio is a jam-packed bar serving good tapas, salads, *huevos estrellados* (scrambled eggs with fried potatoes), and wine. If you'd like to make it a sit-down meal, head to the tables in the back. Their basement is much less atmospheric (Calle Cava Baja 30, tel. 913-662-984).

El Madroño ("The Berry Tree," a symbol of Madrid) is more of a cowboy bar a block off the top of Calle Cava Baja. Preserving a bit of old Madrid, a tile copy of Velázquez's famous *Drinkers* grins from its facade. Inside, look above the stairs for photos of 1902 Madrid. Study the coats of arms of Madrid through the centuries as you try a *vermut* (vermouth) on tap and a €2 sandwich. Or ask to try the *licor de madroño;* a small glass *(chupito)* costs €1.50. While indoor seating is bright and colorful, the sidewalk tables come with great people-watching. Munch *raciones* at bar or front tables to be in the fun scene or have a quieter sit-down meal at the tables in the back (closed Mon, Plaza de la Puerta Cerrada 7, tel. 913-645-629).

Ice Cream Finale: **Giangrossi Helado Artesanal,** a popular chain, serves Argentinean-style ice cream, considered to be some of Madrid's best. With a plush white leather lounge and lots of great flavors, this hipster ice cream shop offers a sweet way to finish your dining experience in this area (at the end of Calle Cava Baja at #40, 50 yards from La Latina Metro stop, tel. 902-444-130).

Near Plaza Santa Ana
Fine Dining
El Caldero ("The Pot") is romantic and *the* place for paella and other rice dishes. A classy, in-the-know local crowd appreciates the subdued elegance and crisp service of this place. The house specialty is *arroz caldero* (a variation on paella). Served with panache from a cauldron hanging from a tripod, it serves two for €28. Most of the formal rice dishes come in pots for two—like the €30-per-couple paella (closed Sun–Mon, Calle de las Huertas 15, tel. 914-295-044). Wash down your meal with the house sangria.

The Madrid Pub-Crawl Dinner (for Beginners)
For maximum fun, people, and atmosphere, go mobile for dinner: Do the "tapas tango," a local tradition of going from one bar to the next, munching, drinking, and socializing. While tiny €2 plates

(tapas) are standard in Andalucía (and commonly served in Madrid's Calle Cava Baja area), these days most of Madrid's bars offer bigger €6 plates called *raciones,* ideal for a small group to share. The real action begins late (around 20:00). But for beginners, an earlier start, with less commotion, can be easier. The litter on the floor is normal; that's where people traditionally toss their trash and shells (it's unsanitary to put it back on the bar). Don't worry about paying until you're ready to go. Then ask for *la cuenta* (the bill).

If done properly, a pub crawl can be a highlight of your trip. Your ability to speak a little Spanish will get you a much better (and less expensive) experience.

Prowl the area between Puerta del Sol and Plaza Santa Ana. There's no ideal route, but the little streets (in this book's map) between Puerta del Sol, San Jerónimo, and Plaza Santa Ana hold tasty surprises. Nearby, the street Jesús de Medinaceli is also lined with popular tapas bars. Below is a five-stop tapa crawl. These places are good, but don't be afraid to make some discoveries of your own. The more adventurous should read this crawl for ideas, and skip directly to the advanced zone (Lavapiés), described at the end of this section. For a more trendy pub crawl with designer tapas and finer wine, visit the bars on Calle Cava Baja (listed earlier).

• *From Puerta del Sol, walk east a block down Carrera de San Jerónimo to the corner of Calle Victoria.*

Museo del Jamón (Museum of Ham): This frenetic, cheap, stand-up bar (with famously rude service) is an assembly line of

MADRID

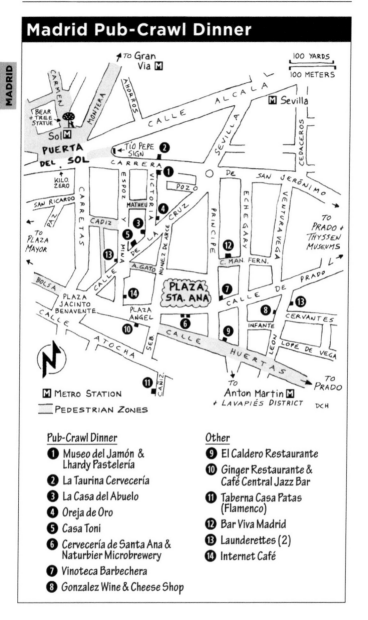

Madrid Pub-Crawl Dinner

Pub-Crawl Dinner
1. Museo del Jamón & Lhardy Pastelería
2. La Taurina Cervecería
3. La Casa del Abuelo
4. Oreja de Oro
5. Casa Toni
6. Cervecería de Santa Ana & Naturbier Microbrewery
7. Vinoteca Barbechera
8. Gonzalez Wine & Cheese Shop

Other
9. El Caldero Restaurante
10. Ginger Restaurante & Café Central Jazz Bar
11. Taberna Casa Patas (Flamenco)
12. Bar Viva Madrid
13. Launderettes (2)
14. Internet Café

fast and simple *bocadillos* and *raciones*. It's tastefully decorated—unless you're a pig (or a vegetarian). Take advantage of the easy photo-illustrated menus that show various dishes and their prices. The best ham is the pricey *jamón ibérico*—from pigs who led stress-free lives in acorn-strewn valleys. Just point and eat, but be specific: A plate of low-end *jamón blanco* costs only €2.50, while *jamón ibérico* costs €14. For a small sandwich, ask for a *chiquito* (€1, or €4 for *ibérico*). If on a budget, don't let them sell you the *ibérico* (daily 9:00–24:00, sit-down restaurant upstairs, air-con).

• *Nearby are two options. Across the street is the touristy and over-priced bull bar, La Taurina. (I wouldn't eat here but you're welcome to ponder the graphic photos that celebrate the gory art of bullfighting.) And next door, take a detour from your pub crawl with something better for grandmothers:*

Lhardy Pastelería: Offering a genteel taste of Old World charm in this district of rowdy pubs, this place has been a fixture since 1839 for Madrileños wanting to duck in for a cup of soup or a light snack. Step right in, and pretend you're an aristocrat back between the wars. Serve yourself. You'll pay as you leave (on the honor system). Help yourself to the silver water dispenser (free), a line of elegant bottles (each a different Iberian fortified wine: sherry, port, and so on, €2/glass), a revolving case of meaty little pastries (€1 each), and a fancy soup dispenser (chicken broth consommé-€2, or €2.50 with a splash of sherry...local style—bottles in the corner, help yourself; Mon–Sat 9:30–15:00 & 17:00–21:30, Sun 9:30–15:00 only, non-smoking, Carrera de San Jerónimo 8).

• *Next, forage halfway up Calle Victoria to the tiny...*

La Casa del Abuelo: This is where seafood-lovers savor sizzling plates of tasty little *gambas* (shrimp) and *langostinos* (prawns), with bread to sop up the delightful juices. As drinks are cheap and

dishes are pricey, you might want to just share a *ración*. Try *gambas a la plancha* (grilled shrimp, €7.60) or *gambas al ajillo* (ah-HEE-yoh, shrimp version of escargot, cooked in oil and garlic, €8.30) and a €2 glass of sweet red house wine (daily 12:00–24:00, Calle Victoria 12).

• *Across the street is...*

Oreja de Oro: The "Golden Ear" is named for what it sells—sautéed pigs' ears (*oreja*, €3). While pig ears are a Madrid specialty, this place is Galician, so people also come here for *pulpo* (octopus, €12), *pimientos de padrón* (sautéed miniature green peppers—my favorite plate of the entire crawl, €3.50), and the distinctive *ribeiro* (ree-BAY-roh) wine, served Galician-style, in characteristic little ceramic bowls (to disguise its lack of clarity). Jaime is a frantic one-man show who somehow gets everything just right (closed Mon). Have fun here.

• *For a finale, continue uphill and around the corner to...*

Casa Toni: This memorable little spot, run by Toni, has a helpful English menu and several fun, classic dishes to try: *patatas bravas* (fried potatoes in a spicy sauce, €4), *berenjena* (deep-fried slices of eggplant, €5), *champiñones* (sautéed mushrooms, €5.50), and gazpacho—the cold tomato-and-garlic soup (€2.50) which is generally served only during the hot season, but available here year-round just for you (closed July, Calle Cruz 14).

More Options: If you're hungry for more, and want a trendy, up-to-date, pricier tapas scene, head for Plaza Santa Ana, with lively bars spilling out onto the square. Survey the entire scene. Consider **Cervecería de Santa Ana** (tasty tapas with two zones: rowdy, circa-1900 beer-hall and classier sit-down) or **Naturbier,** a local microbrewery. **Vinoteca Barbechera,** at the downhill end of the square, has an inviting menu of tapas and fine wines by the glass (indoor and outdoor seating).

Gonzalez, a venerable gourmet cheese and wine shop with a circa 1930s interior, offers a genteel opportunity to enjoy a plate of first-class cheese and a fine glass of wine with friendly service and a fun setting. Their €13 assortment of five Spanish cheeses—more than enough for two—is a cheese-lover's treat (€10 lunch buffet, nice wines by the glass, closed Sun–Mon, three blocks past Plaza Santa Ana at Calle de León 12, tel. 914-295-618, Francisco).

Near the Royal Palace

Casa Ciriaco is popular with Madrileños who appreciate good traditional cooking—stews and partridge—with no affectation (€35 meals, €20 fixed-price lunch and dinner, closed Wed and Aug, Calle Mayor 84, tel. 915-480-620). It was from this building in 1906 that an anarchist bombed the royal couple on their wedding day. Photos of the carnage are inside the front door.

La Bola Taberna, touristy but friendly and tastefully elegant, specializes in *cocido Madrileño*—Madrid stew. The €19 stew consists of various meats, carrots, and garbanzo beans in earthen jugs. This is a winter dish, prepared here for the tourists. The stew is served as two courses: First you enjoy the broth as a soup, then you dig into the meat and veggies (closed Sun, cash only, midway between Royal Palace and Gran Vía at Calle Bola 5, tel. 915-476-930).

Café de Oriente serves a great three-course lunch special (€13, Mon–Fri, 13:00–16:00 only) in fin-de-siècle elegance immediately across the park from the Royal Palace. While its cafeteria

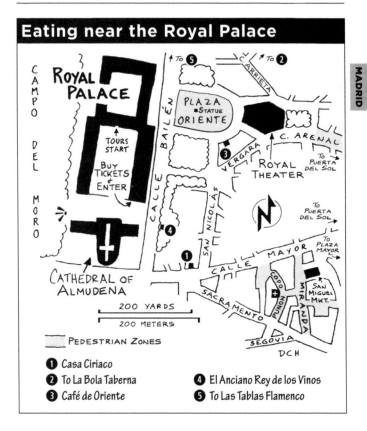

Eating near the Royal Palace

● Casa Ciriaco
● To La Bola Taberna
● Café de Oriente
● El Anciano Rey de los Vinos
● To Las Tablas Flamenco

area is reasonable, its restaurant is pricey (Plaza de Oriente 2, tel. 915-413-974).

El Anciano Rey de los Vinos is a venerable, circa 1909 wine bar famous for its vermouth on tap. It's expensive, but offers affordable tapas and drinks at its classic bar. A free small plate of tapas comes with each drink (closed Tue, across busy street from cathedral at Calle de Bailén 19, tel. 915-595-332).

Casual Dining near the Prado

Each of the three big art museums has a decent cafeteria. Or choose from these eateries, all within a block of the Prado (for locations, see "Madrid's Museum Neighborhood" map).

Taberna de Dolores, a winning formula since 1908, is a commotion of locals enjoying €2.50 *canapés* (open-face sandwiches), tasty *raciones* of seafood, and *cañas* (small beers) at the bar or at a few tables in the back (daily 11:00–24:00, Plaza de Jesús 4, tel. 914-292-243).

VIPS is a bright, popular chain restaurant, handy for a cheap and filling salad. Engulfed in a big bookstore, this is a high-energy, no-charm eatery (daily 9:00–24:00, across the boulevard from northern end of Prado, under Palace Hotel). In 2001, Spain's first Starbucks opened next door.

Viva la Vida Organic Market and Vegetarian Buffet, a tiny deli, offers a take-away buffet that delights vegetarians. Dish up what you like on a paper plate or in a paper box, pay by the weight (€2/100 grams, a plateful is generally 300 grams—about 10 ounces), and grab a nearby bench or hike over to the picnic-friendly Prado Museum grounds or Royal Botanical Garden (daily 11:00–24:00, a few blocks toward the center from the Prado at Calle de las Huertas 57, tel. 913-697-254).

North of Puerta del Sol

Eating Cheaply

Restaurante Puerto Rico fills a long, congested hall by serving good meals for great prices to smart locals (€10 three-course fixed-price meal, closed Sun, Chinchilla 2, between Puerta del Sol and Gran Vía, tel. 915-219-834).

Hotel Europa Cafetería is a fun, high-energy scene with a mile-long bar, old-school waiters, great people-watching, local cuisine, and a fine €11 fixed-price lunch (daily 7:00–24:00, next to Hotel Europa, 50 yards off Puerta del Sol at Calle del Carmen 4, tel. 915-212-900). The menu lists three price levels: bar (inexpensive), table (generally pricey), or terrace (sky-high but with good people-watching). Your best value is to stick to the lunch menu if you're sitting inside, or order off the plastic *barra* menu if you sit at the bar (their €3 ham-and-egg toast makes a nice breakfast).

El Corte Inglés' seventh-floor cafeteria is fresh, modern, and—while not particularly cheap—popular with locals (Mon–Sat 10:00–22:00, closed Sun, non-smoking section, just off Puerta del Sol at intersection of Preciados and Tetuán).

Casa Labra Taberna Restaurante is famous as the birthplace of the Spanish Socialist Party in 1879...and as a spot for great cod. Packed with Madrileños, it manages to be both dainty and rustic. It's a wonderful scene with three distinct sections: the stand-up bar (cheapest, with two lines: one for munchies, the other for drinks), a peaceful little sit-down area in back (a little more expensive but still cheap; €6 salads), and a fancy restaurant (€20 lunches). Their tasty little €1.25 *tajada de bacalao* cod dishes put them on the map. The waiters are fun to joke around with (daily 11:00–15:30 & 18:00–23:00, a block off Puerta del Sol at Calle Tetuán 12, tel. 915-310-081).

La Gloria de Montera Restaurante, a hip Spanish bistro

Breakfast in Madrid

As most hotels don't include breakfast (and many don't even serve it), you may be out on the streets first thing looking for a place. Non-touristy places only offer a hot drink and a pastry, with perhaps a potato omelet and sandwiches (toasted cheese, ham, or both). Touristy places will have a *desayuno* menu with various ham-and-eggs deals. Try *churros* once (see the listings for my favorite places). Starbucks, a temptation for many due to its familiarity, is always nearby. Get advice from your hotel staff for their favorite breakfast place.

with white tablecloths and a minimalist-library ambience, serves mediocre food to locals at a cheap price (€8-10 fish and meat plates, daily, no reservations—arrive early or put your name on the list, a block from Gran Vía at Caballero de Gracia 10, tel. 915-234-407). **Ginger Restaurante,** a twin with the same menu and formula and a little more comfortable seating, is just off Plaza Santa Ana (on Calle de las Huertas at Plaza del Ángel 12, tel. 913-691-059).

Fresc Co is the place for a cheap, modern, fast, and buffet-style meal. It's a chain with a winning plan: a long, appealing salad and buffet bar with one cheap price for all-you-can-eat, including dessert, a drink, and unlimited refills on everything (€9 lunch, €10 dinner, daily 12:30–24:00, air-con, Caballero de Gracia 8, tel. 915-216-052).

Vegetarian: **Artemisia II** is a hit with vegetarians who like good, healthy food in a smoke-free room without the typical hippie ambience that comes with most veggie places (great €11.25 three-course fixed-price lunch Mon–Fri only, open daily 13:30–16:00 & 21:00–24:00, 2 blocks north of Puerta del Sol at Tres Cruces 4, a few steps off Plaza del Carmen, tel. 915-218-721). **Artemisia I,** II's older sister, is located two blocks east of Plaza Santa Ana at Ventura de la Vega 4, off San Jerónimo (same hours, tel. 914-295-092).

Fast Food and Picnics

Fast Food: For an easy, light, cheap meal, try **Rodilla**—a popular sandwich and salad chain with a shop on the northeast corner of Puerta del Sol at #13 (daily 9:30–23:00). **Pans & Company,** with shops throughout Madrid and Spain, offers healthy, tasty sandwiches and pre-packaged salads (daily 9:00–24:00, locations at Puerta del Sol, on Plaza Callao, at Gran Vía 30, and many more).

Picnics: The department store **El Corte Inglés** has well-stocked meat and cheese counters downstairs (Mon–Sat 10:00–22:00, Sun 11:00–21:00).

Churros con Chocolate

Those not watching their cholesterol will want to try the deep-fried doughy treats called *churros* (or the thicker *porras*), best enjoyed by dipping them in pudding-like hot chocolate. While many *chocolaterías* offer the dunkable fritters, *churros* are most delicious when consumed fresh out of the greasy cauldron at a place that actually fries them.

Chocolaterías Valor is a modern chain that does *churros* with pride and gusto. A few minutes' walk from nearly all my hotel recommendations, it's a fine place for breakfast. With a website like www.amigosdelchocolate.com, you know where their heart is (€4 *churros con chocolate,* daily 8:00–22:30, Fri–Sat until 24:00, a half-block below Plaza Callao and Gran Vía at Postigo de San Martín 7, tel. 915-229-288).

Chocolatería San Ginés is a classy institution, much beloved by Madrileños for its *churros con chocolate* (€4). Dunk your *churros* into the chocolate pudding, as locals have done here for more than 100 years. While quiet before midnight, it's packed with the disco crowd in the wee hours; the popular dance club Joy Eslava is next door (open 21 hours a day—it's only closed between 6:30–9:30; from Puerta del Sol, take Calle del Arenal 2 blocks west, turn left on bookstore-lined Pasadizo de San Ginés, and you'll see the café—it's at #5; tel. 913-656-546).

The Lavapiés District Tapas Crawl (for the Adventurous)

The neighborhood called Lavapiés is emerging as a colorful magnet for people-watching. This is where the multi-ethnic tapestry of Madrid society enjoys pithy, cheap, seedy-yet-fun-loving life on the streets. Neighborhoods like this typically experience an evolution: initially they're so cheap that only the immigrants, downtrodden, and counter-culture types live there. The diversity and color they bring attracts those with more money. Businesses erupt to cater to those bohemian/trendy tastes. Rents go up. Those who gave the area the colorful liveliness in the first place can no longer afford to live there. They move out...and here comes Starbucks. For now, Lavapiés is still edgy, yet comfortable enough for most.

This district has almost no tourists. (It's too scary.) Old ladies with their tired bodies and busy fans hang out on their tiny balconies as they have for 40 years, watching the scene. Shady types lurk on side streets (don't venture off the main drag, don't show your wallet or money, and don't linger on Plaza Lavapiés).

For food, you'll find all the various kinds of tapas bars described earlier in "The Madrid Pub-Crawl Dinner (for Beginners)," plus great Indian (almost all run by Bangladeshis) and Moroccan eateries. I've listed a couple of places that appealed to me...but explore your options. I'd recommend taking the entire walk once, then backtracking and eating at the place or places that appeal to you.

From the Antón Martín Metro stop (or Plaza Santa Ana), walk down Calle Ave María (on its way to becoming Calle Ave Allah) to Plaza Lavapiés (where old ladies hang out with the swarthy drunks and a mosaic of cultures treat this square as a communal living room; Metro station here), and then up Calle de Lavapiés to the newly remodeled square, Plaza Tirso de Molina (Metro stop). This square was once plagued by druggies. Now with flower kiosks and a playground, it's homey and inviting. This is a fine example of the new vision for Madrid's public spaces.

On Calle Ave María: **Bar Melos** is a thriving dive jammed with a hungry and nubile local crowd. It's famous for its giant patty melts called *zapatillas de lacón y queso* (because they're the size and shape of a *zapatilla* or slipper, €7, feeds at least two, Ave María 44, smoky tables in back). **Nuevo Café Barbieri,** one of a dying breed of smoky mirrored cafés with a circa-1940 ambience, offers classical music in the afternoon and jazz in the evening (Ave María 45).

On Calle de Lavapiés: At Calle de Lavapiés 44, consider an Indian place or drop into **Montes Wine Bar** (countless wines open and served by the glass, good tapas, crawl under the bar to get to the WC).

Connections

By Train

Remember that Madrid has two main train stations: Chamartín and Atocha. At the Atocha Station, AVE and other long-distance trains depart from a different area than local *cercanías* trains (for more details, see "Arrival in Madrid").

AVE Trains: Spain's AVE (AH-vay) bullet train opens up some good itinerary options. You can now get from Madrid's Atocha Station to **Barcelona** in three hours, with trains running almost hourly. The AVE train is generally faster (timed from downtown to downtown) and easier than flying, but not necessarily cheaper. Basic second-class tickets are €110 one-way for most departures and €130 for the fastest, peak-time departures. First-class tickets are €180. Advance purchase discounts (40–60 days ahead) are available through the national rail company (RENFE), but sell out quickly. Save by not traveling on holidays.

The AVE is also handy for visiting **Sevilla** (and, on the way, **Córdoba**). The basic Madrid–Sevilla second-class AVE fare is €70–80, depending upon departure time; first-class AVE costs €140 and comes with a meal). Consider this exciting day trip to Sevilla from Madrid: 7:00–depart Madrid, 8:45–12:40–in Córdoba, 13:30–20:45–in Sevilla, 23:30–back in Madrid.

MADRID

Other AVE destinations include **Toledo** (nearly hourly, 30 min, €10, from Atocha) and **Segovia** (8/day, 35 min, €10, from Chamartín Station, take train going toward Valladolid). For the latest, pick up the AVE brochure at the station, or check out www .renfe.es/ave. Prices vary with times and class. Eurailpass-holders get a big discount (e.g., Madrid to Sevilla is €9 second-class, but only at RENFE ticket windows—discount not available at ticket machines). Reserve each AVE segment ahead (tel. 902-240-202 for Atocha AVE info).

Below I've listed both non-AVE and (where available) AVE trains, to help you compare your options.

From Madrid by Train to: Toledo (AVE: nearly hourly, 30 min, from Atocha), **El Escorial** (1–2/hr, but bus is better), **Segovia** (AVE: 8/day, 35 min plus 20-min shuttle bus into Segovia center, from Chamartín; slower *cercanías* trains: 9/day, 2 hrs, from both Chamartín and Atocha), **Ávila** (hourly until 21:30, 90 min, more departures from Chamartín than Atocha), **Salamanca** (7/day, 2.5 hrs, from Chamartín), **Santiago de Compostela** (2/day, 8–9.5 hrs, includes night train, from Chamartín), **Barcelona** (AVE: almost hourly, 3 hrs from Atocha; plus 1 night train from Chamartín, 9 hrs), **San Sebastián** (3/day, 5–6 hrs, from Atocha or Chamartín), **Pamplona** (4/day direct, 3 hrs, from Atocha), **Burgos** (7/day, 5 hrs, from Chamartín), **León** (11/day, 4 hrs, from Chamartín), **Granada** (2/day, 5 hrs, from Atocha), **Sevilla** (AVE: hourly, 2.5 hrs, departures from 16:00–19:00 can sell out far in advance, from Atocha), **Córdoba** (AVE: 28/day, 1.75 hrs; Altaria trains: 5/day, 2 hrs; all from Atocha), **Málaga** (AVE: 12/day, 2.5–3 hrs, from Atocha), **Algeciras** (Altaria trains: 2/day, 5.5 hrs, from Atocha), **Lisbon** (1/day departing at 22:45, 9 hrs, overnight Hotel Train from Chamartín), **Paris** (1/day, 13 hrs, direct overnight—a €185 Hotel Train, reserve more than 15 days in advance and hope there are seats left in the €89 *oferta mini* deals, from Chamartín). General train info: tel. 902-240-202, for international journeys: tel. 902-243-402, www.renfe.es.

By Bus

Madrid has several major bus stations, connected by Metro. If you take a taxi to any bus station, you'll be charged a legitimate €3 supplement. Buses to **Toledo** run from the bus station at Plaza Elíptica (2/hr, 1–1.5 hrs, €5 one-way, *directo* faster than *ruta*, Continental Auto bus company, tel. 915-272-961, Metro: Plaza Elíptica).

Estación Sur de Autobuses (South Bus Station): From here, you can catch buses to **Ávila** (8/day, 1.5 hrs, €13 round-trip), **Salamanca** (hourly express, 2.5 hrs, €20 one-way, tel. 902-020-052, www.avanzabus.com), **León** (10/day, 4 hrs, €21 one-way),

Santiago de Compostela (5/day, 8 hrs, includes 24:30–9:00 night bus), and **Granada** (18/day, 5.25 hrs, €16 one-way, tel. 915-272-961). The station sits squarely on top of Metro: Méndez Álvaro (has TI, tel. 914-684-200, www.estacionautobusesmadrid.com).

Príncipe Pío Station: Príncipe Pío is the old North train station, which has now morphed into a trendy mall and a bus hub for local lines including **Segovia** (€7 one-way, €12 round-trip, 2/hr departing on half-hour from platforms 6 or 7, 1.25 hrs, Mon–Sat first departure at 6:30, last return at 21:30, Sun first 8:30 and last 22:30). From Metro: Príncipe Pío, follow signs to *terminal de autobuses* or follow pictures of a bus (tel. 915-598-955, www.la sepulvedana.es). Buy a ticket from the Sepulvedana window (platform 4). Reservations are rarely necessary.

Intercambiador de Moncloa Station: This station, in the Moncloa Metro station, serves **El Escorial** (4/hr, 45–55 min). To reach the **Valley of the Fallen,** you'll first go to El Escorial, then connect on the bus from there (1/day Tue–Sun only, 15 min from El Escorial).

Intercambiador de Avenida de América Station: Located at the Avenida de América Metro, buses go to **Burgos** (9/day, 3 hrs) and **Pamplona** (6/day, 5 hrs, Alsa, tel. 915-272-961, www.movelia.es).

Route Tips for Drivers

Avoid driving in Madrid. Rent your car when you depart. To leave Madrid from Gran Vía, simply follow signs for *A-6* (direction *Villalba* or *A Coruña*) for Segovia, El Escorial, or the Valley of the Fallen (see next chapter for details).

It's cheapest to make car-rental arrangements before you leave home. In Madrid, consider **Europcar** (central reservations tel. 902-105-030, San Leonardo 8 office tel. 915-418-892, Chamartín Station tel. 913-231-721, airport tel. 913-937-235), **Hertz** (central reservations tel. 902-402-405, Plaza de España 18 tel. 915-425-805, Chamartín Station tel. 917-330-400, airport tel. 913-937-228), **Avis** (central reservations tel. 902-200-162, Gran Vía 60 tel. 915-484-204, airport tel. 913-937-223), and **National Atesa** (central reservations tel. 902-100-515). Ask about free delivery to your hotel. At the airport, most rental cars are returned at Terminal 1.

Madrid's Barajas Airport

Ten miles east of downtown, Madrid's modern airport has four terminals. Terminals 1, 2, and 3 are connected by long indoor walkways (about an 8-min walk apart), and serve airlines including Continental, Delta, Northwest, United, US Airways, Air Canada, and Spanair. The newer Terminal 4 serves airlines including Iberia, Vueling, British, and American, and also has a separate satellite terminal called T4S. To transfer between Terminals 1–3 and Terminal 4, you can take a 10-minute shuttle bus (free, leaves every 10 min from departures level), or take the Metro (stops at Terminals 2 and 4). Make sure to allow enough time if you need to travel between terminals (and then for the long walk within Terminal 4 to the gates). For more information about navigating this massive airport, go to www.aena.es.

International flights typically use Terminals 1 and 4. At the Terminal 1 arrivals area, you'll find a helpful English-speaking **TI** (marked *Oficina de Información Turística*, Mon–Sat 8:00–20:00, Sun 9:00–14:00, tel. 913-058-656); **ATMs;** a **flight info office** (marked simply *Information* in airport lobby, open daily 24 hours, tel. 902-353-570); a **post-office** window; a **pharmacy;** lots of **phones** (buy a phone card from the nearby machine); a few scattered **Internet** terminals (small fee); **eateries;** a **RENFE office** (where you can get train info and buy long-distance train tickets, daily 8:00–21:00, tel. 902-240-202); and on-the-spot **car-rental agencies** (see previous page). The new super-modern Terminal 4 offers essentially the same services.

Iberia, Spanair, and Air Europa are Spain's airlines, connecting a reasonable number of cities in Spain, as well as international destinations (ask for best rates at travel agencies). Vueling is the most popular discount airline in Iberia (e.g., Madrid–Barcelona flight as cheap as €30 if booked in advance, tel. 902-333-933, www .vueling.com).

Getting Between the Airport and Downtown

By Public Bus: Bus #200 shuttles travelers between airport Terminals 1, 2, and 3 (departing from arrivals level every 10 minutes, runs 6:00–24:00) and the Metro stop Avenida de América (northeast of the historical center) in about 20 minutes. From that Metro stop, you can connect to your hotel by taking the Metro or hopping a taxi. Bus #204 serves Terminal 4 the same way. The trip costs only €1 (buy ticket from driver; or get a shareable 10-ride Metrobus ticket for €7.40 at a tobacco shop—for more info, see "Getting Around Madrid").

By Metro: The subway involves two transfers to reach the city center (€2; or add a €1 supplement to your €7.40 10-ride Metrobus ticket). The airport's futuristic "Aeropuerto T-1, T-2, T-3" Metro stop (notice the ATMs, subway info booth, and huge lighted map of Madrid) is in Terminal 2. Access the Metro at the check-in level; to reach the Metro from Terminal 1's arrivals level, stand with your back to the baggage claim, then go to your far right, up the stairs, and follow red-and-blue Metro diamond signs to the station (8-min walk). The Terminal 4 stop is the end of the line. To get to Puerta del Sol, take line 8 for 12 minutes to Nuevos

Ministerios, then continue on line 10 to Tribunal, then line 1 to Puerta del Sol (30 min more total); or exit at Nuevos Ministerios and take a €5 taxi or bus #150 straight to Puerta del Sol.

By Minibus Shuttle: The AeroCity shuttle bus provides door-to-door transport in a seven-seat minibus with up to three hotel stops en route. It's promoted by hotels, but if you want door-to-door service, simply taking a taxi generally offers a better value.

By Taxi: Considering the speed, ease, and economy of riding the subway in from the airport, I'd opt for the Metro over taxis. If you take a taxi between the airport and downtown, allow about €25 during the day *(Tarifa 1)* or €35 at night and on Sundays *(Tarifa 2)*. For Terminal 4, add about €10. Insist on the meter. The €5 airport supplement is legal. There is no charge for luggage. Plan on getting stalled in traffic.

NORTHWEST OF MADRID

El Escorial • Valley of the Fallen • Segovia • Ávila

Before slipping out of Madrid, consider several fine side-trips northwest of Spain's capital city, all conveniently reached by car, bus, or train.

Spain's lavish, brutal, and complicated history is revealed throughout Old Castile. This region, where the Spanish language originated, is named for its many castles—battle scars from the long-fought Reconquista.

An hour from Madrid, tour the imposing and fascinating palace at El Escorial, headquarters of the Spanish Inquisition. Nearby at the awe-inspiring Valley of the Fallen, pay tribute to the countless victims of Spain's bloody civil war.

Segovia, with its remarkable Roman aqueduct (pictured above) and romantic castle, is another worthwhile side-trip. At Ávila, you can walk the perfectly preserved medieval walls.

Planning Your Time

See El Escorial and the Valley of the Fallen together in less than a day (but not on Monday, when both sights are closed). By car, do them en route to Segovia; by bus, make it a day trip from Madrid.

Segovia is worth a half-day of sightseeing and is a joy at night. Ávila, while it has its charm, merits only a quick stop (if you're driving and in the area, 1.5 hours from Madrid, also a logical stop on the way to Salamanca by train) to marvel at its medieval walls and, perhaps, check out St. Teresa's finger.

In total, these sights are worth two days if you're in Spain for less than a month. If you're a history buff in Spain for just a week, squeeze in a quick side-trip from Madrid to El Escorial and the Valley of the Fallen.

Northwest of Madrid

El Escorial

The Monasterio de San Lorenzo de El Escorial is a symbol of power rather than elegance. This 16th-century palace, 30 miles northwest of Madrid, gives us a better feel for the Counter-Reformation and the Inquisition than any other building.

Getting to El Escorial

Most people visit El Escorial from Madrid. By public transportation, the bus is most convenient (since it gets you closer to the palace). Remember that it makes sense to combine El Escorial with a visit to the nearby Valley of the Fallen (also described in this chapter).

Cheap Tricks

At El Escorial
Download and print out a free detailed English guide of three architectural and historic tours through San Lorenzo de El Escorial by clicking on the "Place for walks" link at www.san lorenzoturismo.org.

In Segovia
Segovia has plenty of little Romanesque churches that are free to enter, and many have architecturally interesting exteriors that are worth a look. On your way to the main sights, keep your eyes peeled for these hidden treasures: Coming from the bus station on Avenida de Fernández Ladreda toward the center of town, you can see the San Millán church; on Plazas San Martín and San Esteban are two churches sharing their squares' names; and on the way to the Alcázar on Plaza de la Merced is the San Andrés church.

In Ávila
As you're wandering the city and you see the arched gates leading out of the old center, pop out to the other side and take in the impressive wall. Exploring sections of it from the ground may be even better than walking along it, and saves you the admission fee.

By Bus: Buses leave from the Intercambiador de Moncloa, which is in the basement of Madrid's Moncloa Metro stop (4/ hr, fewer on weekends, 45–55 min, €3.40 one-way, buy ticket from driver; in Madrid take bus #664 or slower #661 from Intercambiador's platform 3, Herranz Bus, tel. 918-969-028). The bus drops you downtown in San Lorenzo de El Escorial, a pleasant 10-minute stroll from the palace (see map): Exit the bus station from the back ramp that leads over the parked buses, turn left, and follow the newly cobbled pedestrian lane, Calle San Juan. This street veers to the right and becomes Calle Juan de Leyra. In a few short blocks, it dead-ends at Duque de Medinaceli, where you'll turn left and see the palace. Stairs lead past several decent eateries, through a delightful park, past the TI (Mon–Fri 10:00–18:00, Sat–Sun 10:00–19:00, tel. 918-905-313), and directly to the tourist entry of the immense palace/monastery.

By Train: Local trains (*cercanías* line C-8A) run once or twice an hour from Madrid's Atocha and Chamartín Stations to El Escorial. From the station, walk 20 minutes uphill through Casita del Príncipe park, straight up from the station. Or you can take a shuttle bus (2/hr, €1) or a taxi (€5) to the San Lorenzo de El Escorial town center and the palace.

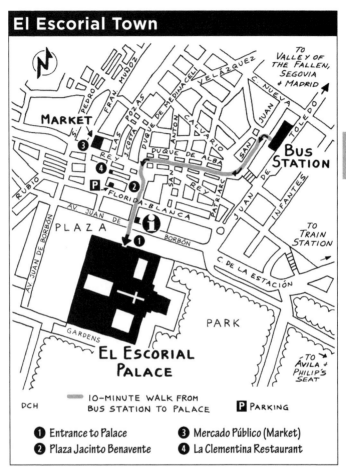

El Escorial Town

MARKET

BUS STATION

PLAZA

EL ESCORIAL PALACE

PARK

GARDENS

TO VALLEY OF THE FALLEN, SEGOVIA & MADRID

TO TRAIN STATION

TO ÁVILA & PHILIP'S SEAT

C. DE LA ESTACIÓN

BORBÓN

FLORIDA-BLANCA

AV. JUAN DE BORBÓN

DCH

🚶 10-MINUTE WALK FROM BUS STATION TO PALACE   🅿 PARKING

❶ Entrance to Palace   ❸ Mercado Público (Market)
❷ Plaza Jacinto Benavente   ❹ La Clementina Restaurant

NORTHWEST OF MADRID

By Car: It's quite simple. Taxi to your car-rental office in Madrid (or ask if they'll deliver the car to your hotel). Pick up the car by 8:30 and ask for directions to highway A-6. From Gran Vía in central Madrid, follow signs to *A-6* (direction *Villalba* or *A Coruña*). The freeway leads directly out of town. Stay on A-6 past the first El Escorial exit. At kilometer 37, you'll see the cross marking the Valley of the Fallen ahead on the left. Exit 47 takes you to both the Valley of the Fallen (after a half-mile, a granite gate on right marks Valle de los Caídos turn-off) and El Escorial (follow *San Lorenzo del Escorial* signs).

The nearby **Silla de Felipe** (Philip's Seat) is a rocky viewpoint where the king would come to admire his palace as it was being built. From El Escorial, follow directions to Ávila, then M-505 to Valdemorillo; look for a sign on your right after about a mile.

When you leave El Escorial for Madrid, Toledo, or Segovia, follow signs to *A-6 Guadarrama*. After about six miles, you pass the Valley of the Fallen and hit the freeway.

Sights

▲▲▲Monasterio de San Lorenzo de El Escorial

Built at a time when Catholic Spain felt threatened by Protestant "heretics," the construction of this palace dominated the Spanish economy for a generation (1562–1584). Because of this bully in the national budget, Spain has almost nothing else to show from this most powerful period of her history.

Cost: The basic, unguided €8 *visita libre* ticket lets you tour the complex on your own (or with the help of a rentable audio-guide—see below; with this ticket the Royal Pantheon crypt is off-limits unless you rent an audioguide). The €10 *visita guiada* **ticket** includes a guided tour (ask for next tour in English; only sold until 90 min before closing time). If you're also going to the Valley of the Fallen, the **combo-ticket** sold here will save you some euros (€8.50 includes unguided El Escorial visit, €11 includes guided El Escorial visit, sold before 15:00 April–Sept or before 14:00 Oct–March).

Hours: April–Sept Tue–Sun 10:00–19:00, Oct–March until 18:00, always closed Mon, last entry one hour before closing, last English tour 90 min before closing.

Information: You'll find scant captions in English within the palace—if you want to visit on your own, you can take my self-guided tour (see below), which covers the basics. For more information, get the *Guide: Monastery of San Lorenzo El Real de El Escorial,* which follows the general route you'll take (€8, available at any of several shops in the palace). The audioguide rents for €2.30 (or pay €3 to get a voucher for an audioguide at the Valley of the Fallen as well). Tel. 918-905-904.

❍ Self-Guided Tour: The *monasterio* looks confusing at first, but the *visita* arrows and signs guide you clearly through one continuous path. This is the general order you'll follow.

Pass through the security scanner, buy your ticket, and then continue down the hall past the *consigna* baggage check (Sala 1) to the **Chamber of the Honor Guards.** This chamber is hung with 16th-century tapestries, including fascinating copies of Hieronymus Bosch's most famous and preachy paintings (which Philip II fancied). Don't miss El Greco's towering painting of the *Martyrdom of St. Maurice.* This was the artist's first commission after arriving in Spain from Venice. It was too subtle and complex for the king, so El Greco moved on to Toledo to find work.

Continue downstairs to the fascinating **Museum of Archi-**

El Escorial—Ground Floor

TO TRAIN STN.

KING'S APARTMENTS (UPPER FLOOR)

GARDENS

WALKING GALLERY

ROYAL PANTHEON
(STAIRS LEAD DOWN TO CRYPT)

MUSEUM OF PAINTINGS

MUSEUM OF ARCHITECTURE

ALTAR (DOME)

PANTHEON OF ROYAL CHILDREN

HALL OF THE BATTLES

TO TOWN, T.I. & BUS STN.

BASILICA

CELLINI'S CHRIST

CHAPTER ROOMS

GARDENS

SHOP

WC

VISITORS' ENTRANCE

START

TICKETS

PATIO OF THE KINGS

MONASTERY (CLOSED TO PUBLIC)

COLLEGE (CLOSED TO PUBLIC)

LIBRARY (UPPER FLOOR)

FINISH

DCH

NORTHWEST OF MADRID

tecture (Museo de Arquitectura). It has long parallel corridors of fine models of the palace and some of the actual machinery and tools used to construct it. Huge stone-pinching winches, fat ropes, and rusty mortar spades help convey the immensity of this 21-year project involving 1,500 workers. At the big model, notice the complex is shaped like a grill, and recall how San Lorenzo—St. Lawrence, a Christian Spaniard martyred by pagan Romans (A.D. 258)—was burned to death on a grill. Throughout the palace, you'll see this symbol associated with the saint. The grill's "handle" was the palace, or residence of the royal family. The monastery and school gathered around the huge basilica.

Next, linger in the **Museum of Paintings** to consider the 15th- to 17th-century Flemish, Spanish, and Italian works. Contemplate Roger van der Weyden's *Calvary,* with mourning Mary and St. John at the feet of the crucified Christ. (It's interesting to compare it with van der Weyden's similar *Descent from the Cross,* which hangs in the Prado in Madrid.) Then pass through the peaceful and empty Courtyard of Masks to reach the **Hall of Battles** (Sala de Batallas). Its paintings celebrate Spain's great military victories—including the Battle of San Quentin over France (1557) on St. Lawrence's feast day, which inspired the construction of El Escorial. The sprawling series, painted in 1590, helped teach the

History of El Escorial

The giant, gloomy building made of gray-black stone looks more like a prison than a palace. About 650 feet long and 500 feet wide, it has 2,600 windows, 1,200 doors, more than 100 miles of passages, and 1,600 overwhelmed tourists.

Four hundred years ago, the enigmatic, introverted, and extremely Catholic King Philip II (1527–1598) ruled his bulky empire and directed the Inquisition from here. To Philip, the building embodied the wonders of Catholic learning, spirituality, and arts. To 16th-century followers of Martin Luther, it epitomized the evil of closed-minded Catholicism. To architects, the building—built on the cusp between styles— exudes both Counter-Reformation grandeur and understated Renaissance simplicity. Today, it's a time capsule of Spain's "Golden Age," packed with history, art, and Inquisition ghosts. (And at an elevation of nearly 3,500 feet, it can be friggin' cold.)

The building was conceived by Philip II to serve several purposes: as a grand mausoleum for Spain's royal family, starting with his father, Charles V (known as Carlos I in Spain); as a monastery to pray (a lot) for the royal souls; as a small palace to use as a Camp David of sorts for Spain's royalty; and as a school to embrace humanism in a way that promoted the Catholic faith.

new king all the elements of warfare. Stroll the length for a primer on army skills.

From here, a corridor lined with various family trees (some scrawny, others lush and fecund) leads into the royal living quarters (the building's grill handle). Immediately inside the first door, find the small portrait of Philip II flanked by two large portraits of his daughters. The palace was like Philip: austere. Notice the simple floors, plain white walls, and bare-bones chandelier. This was the bedroom of one of his daughters. Notice the sheet warmer beside her bed—often necessary during the winter. Bend down to see the view from her bed...of the high altar in the basilica next door. The entire complex of palace and monastery buildings was built around that altar.

In the next room, the **Guard's room,** notice the reclinable sedan chair that Philip II, thick with gout, was carried in (for seven days) on his last trip from Madrid to El Escorial. He wanted to be here when he died.

The **Audience Chamber** is now a portrait gallery filled with Habsburg royals painted by popular local artists. The portraits of unattractive people that line the walls provide an instructive peek at the consequences of mixing blue blood with more of the same blue blood (inbreeding among royals was a common problem throughout Europe in those days).

The Spanish emperor Charles V (1500–1558) is over the fireplace mantel. Charles, Philip II's dad, was the most powerful man in Europe, having inherited not only the Spanish crown, but also Germany, Austria, the Low Countries (Belgium and the Netherlands), and much of Italy. When he announced his abdication in 1555, his son Philip II inherited much of this territory... plus the responsibility of managing it. Philip's draining wars with France, Portugal, Holland, and England—including the disastrous defeat of Spain's navy, the Spanish Armada, by England's Queen Elizabeth I (1588)—knocked Spain from its peak of power and began centuries of decline.

The guy with the good-looking legs next to Charles was his illegitimate son, Don Juan de Austria—famous for his handsome looks, thanks to a little fresh blood. Other royal offspring weren't so lucky: When one king married his niece, the result was Charles II (1665–1700, opposite Charles V). His severe underbite (an inbred royal family trait) was the least of his problems. An epileptic before that disease was understood, poor "Charles the Mad" would be the last of the Spanish Habsburgs. He died without an heir in 1700, ushering in the continent-wide War of the Spanish Succession and the dismantling of Spain's empire.

In the **Walking Gallery,** the royals got their exercise privately, with no risk of darkening their high-class skins with a tan. Study the 16th-century maps that line the walls. The slate strip on the floor is a sundial from 1755. It lined up with a (now plugged) hole in the wall so that at noon a tiny beam hit the middle of the three lines. Palace clocks were set by this. Where the ray crossed the strip indicated the date and sign of the zodiac.

As you enter the **King's Antechamber,** look back to study the fine inlaid-wood door (a gift from the German emperor that celebrates the exciting humanism of the age).

Philip II's bedroom is austere, like his daughter's. Look at the king's humble bed...barely queen-size. He too could view Mass at the basilica's high altar without leaving his bed. The red box next to his pillow holds the royal bedpan. But don't laugh—the king's looking down from the wall behind you. At age 71, Philip II, the gout-ridden king of a dying empire, died in this bed (1598).

From here, his body was taken to the **Royal Pantheon** (Panteón Real), the gilded resting place of 26 kings and queens... four centuries' worth of Spanish monarchy (a detour on your route, and only accessible if you're on the guided visit or have the audioguide). All the kings are included—but only those queens who became mothers of kings.

There is a post-mortem filing system at work in the Pantheon.

From the entrance, kings are on the left, queens on the right. (The only exception is Isabel II, since she was a ruling queen and her husband was a consort.) The first and greatest, Charles V and his Queen Isabel, flank the altar on the top shelf. Her son, Philip II, rests below Charles and opposite (only) one of Philip's four wives, and so on. There is a waiting process, too. Before a royal corpse can rest in this room, it needs to decompose for several decades. The three empty niches are already booked. The bones of the current king Juan Carlos' grandmother, Victoria Eugenia (who died in 1964), are ready to be moved in, but the staff can't explain why they haven't been transferred yet. Juan Carlos' father, Don Juan (who died in 1993), is also on the waiting list...controversially. Technically, he was never crowned king of Spain—Franco took control of Spain before Don Juan could ascend to the throne, and he was passed over for the job when Franco reinstituted the monarchy. Juan Carlos' mother is the most recent guest in the rotting room. So where does that leave Juan Carlos and Sofía? This hotel is *todo completo*.

The next rooms are filled with the tombs of lesser royals: Each bears that person's name (in Latin), relationship to the king, and slogan or epitaph. From here, it's on to the wedding-cake **Pantheon of Royal Children** (Panteón de los Infantes, accessible with any kind of ticket), which holds the remains of various royal children who died before the age of seven (and their first Communion).

Head past the mini–gift shop and continue upstairs to the **Chapter Rooms** (Salas Capitulares). These rooms, where the monks met to do church business, are lined with big-name paintings by José Ribera, El Greco, Titian, and Velázquez. (More great

paintings are in the monastery's Museum of Painting.) Continue to the final room to see some atypical Bosch paintings and the intricate, portable altar of Charles V. The **cloister** glows with bright, newly restored paintings by Pellegrino Tibaldi. Off the cloister is the **Old Church** (Iglesia Vieja), which they used from 1571 to 1586, while finishing the basilica. During that time, the bodies of several kings, including Charles V, were interred here. Among the many paintings you'll see, look for the powerful *Martyrdom of St. Lawrence* by Tiziano (Titian) above the main altar.

Follow the signs to the **basilica,** which may be closed in 2010 for restoration. If it's open, find the flame-engulfed grill in the center of the altar wall that features San Lorenzo (the same St.

Lawrence from the painting) meeting his famous death—and taking "turn the other cheek" to new extremes. Lorenzo was so cool, he reportedly told his Roman executioners, "You can turn me over now—I'm done on this side." With your back to the altar, go to the right corner for the artistic highlight of the basilica: Benvenuto Cellini's marble sculpture *The Crucifixion*. Jesus' features are supposedly modeled after the Shroud of Turin. Cellini carved this from Carrara marble for his own tomb in 1562 (according to the letters under Christ's feet).

Last comes the immense **library** *(biblioteca)*—where it's clear that education was a priority for the Spanish royalty. Savor this

room. The ceiling (by Tibaldi, depicting various disciplines labeled in Latin, the lingua franca of the multinational Habsburg Empire) is a burst of color. At the far end of the room, the elaborate model of the solar system looks like a giant gyroscope, revolving unmistakably around the Earth, with a misshapen, under-explored North America. As you leave, look back above the wooden door. The plaque warns *"Excomunión..."*—you'll be excommunicated if you take a book without checking it out properly. Who needs late fees when you hold the keys to hell?

Eating in El Escorial

The **Mercado Público,** a four-minute walk from the palace, is the place to shop for a picnic (Mon–Fri 9:30–13:30 & 17:00–20:00, Sat 9:30–14:00, closed Thu and Sat afternoons and all day Sun, Calle del Rey 9).

La Clementina serves appealing tapas at their bar and full meals in the restaurant. In warm weather, their outdoor tables are a treat (daily 13:30–16:30 & 20:30–24:00, Plaza de la Constitución 9, tel. 918-901-192). Other restaurants sell *menú del día* (three-course fixed-price meals) options on nearby squares.

Valley of the Fallen

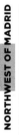

Six miles from El Escorial, high in the Guadarrama Mountains, is the Valley of the Fallen (Valle de los Caídos). A 500-foot-tall granite cross marks this immense and powerful underground monument to the victims of Spain's 20th-century nightmare—its Civil War (1936–1939).

Cost: €5, or €8.30 to include the round-trip bus from El Escorial. But if you're also visiting El Escorial, buy the combo-ticket: €8.50 includes unguided El Escorial visit, €11 includes guided El Escorial visit (sold before 15:00 April–Sept or before 14:00 Oct–March).

Hours: April–Sept Tue–Sun 10:00–19:00, Oct–March until 18:00, closed Mon, last entry one hour before closing, basilica closes 30 min before site closes, tel. 918-905-611.

Getting There: Most visitors side-trip to the Valley of the Fallen from the nearby El Escorial. If you don't have your own wheels, the easiest way to get between these two sights is to negotiate a deal with a **taxi** (to take you from El Escorial to Valley of the Fallen, wait for you 30–60 min, and then bring you back to El Escorial, about €45 total). Otherwise, one **bus** a day (#660) connects El Escorial with the Valley of the Fallen (15 min, leaves El Escorial at 15:15, leaves Valley of the Fallen at 17:30, €8.30 round-trip includes admission to the site, or €4.30 round-trip for just the bus—if you've already bought the Escorial/Valley combo-ticket; no bus on Mon, when both sights are closed). Drivers can find tips under "Getting to El Escorial—By Car."

Audioguide: The audioguide (€2, or included in €3 combo-ticket with El Escorial audioguide) is heavy on the theological message of the statues and tapestries, and it ignores Franco.

➲ **Self-Guided Tour:** Approaching by car or bus, you enter the sprawling park through a granite gate. The best views of the cross are from the bridge (but note that it's illegal for drivers to stop anywhere along this road). To the right, tiny chapels along the ridge mark the Stations of the Cross, where pilgrims stop on their hike to this memorial.

In 1940, prison workers dug 220,000 tons of granite out of the hill beneath the cross to form an underground basilica, then used the stones to erect the cross (built like a chimney, from the inside). Since it's built directly over the dome of the subterranean basilica, a seismologist keeps a careful eye on things.

The Spanish Civil War
(1936–1939)

Thirty-three months of warfare killed 200,000 Spaniards. Unlike America's Civil War, which split America roughly north and south, Spain's war was between classes and ideologies, dividing every city and village, and many families. It was especially cruel, with atrocities and reprisals on both sides.

The war began as a military coup to overthrow the democratically elected Republic, a government that the army and other conservative powers considered too liberal and disorganized. The rebel forces, called the Nationalists *(Nacionalistas)*, consisted of the army, monarchy, Catholic Church, big business, and rural estates, with aid from Germany, Italy, and Portugal. Trying to preserve the liberal government were the Republicans *(Republicanos)*, also called Loyalists: the government, urban areas, secularists, small business, and labor unions, with aid from the United States (minimal help) and the "International Brigades" of communists, socialists, and labor organizers.

In the summer of 1936, the army rebelled and took control of its own garrisons, rejecting the Republic and pledging allegiance to Generalísimo Francisco Franco (1892–1975). These Nationalists launched a three-year military offensive to take Spain region by region, town by town. The government ("Republicans") cobbled together an army of volunteers, local militias, and international fighters. The war pitted conservative Catholic priests against socialist factory workers, rich businessmen against radical students, sunburned farmers loyal to the old king against upwardly mobile small businessmen. People suffered. You'll notice that nearly every Spaniard in his or her 70s is very short—a product of growing up during these hungry and very difficult Civil War years.

Spain's Civil War attracted international attention. Adolf Hitler and Benito Mussolini sent troops and supplies to their fellow fascist, Franco. It was Hitler's Luftwaffe that helped Franco bomb the town of Guernica (April 1937), an event famously captured on canvas by Pablo Picasso. On the Republican side, hundreds of Americans (including Ernest Hemingway) steamed over to Spain, some to fight for democracy as part of the "Abraham Lincoln Brigade."

By 1938, only Barcelona and Madrid held out. But they were no match for Franco's army. On April 1, 1939, Madrid fell and the war ended, beginning 37 years of iron-fisted rule by Franco.

The stairs that lead to the imposing monument are grouped in sets of tens, meant to symbolize the Ten Commandments (including "Thou shalt not kill"—hmm). The emotional *pietà* draped over the basilica's entrance is huge—you could sit in the palm of Christ's hand. The statue was sculpted by Juan de Ávalos, the same artist who created the dramatic figures of the four Evangelists at the base of the cross. It must have had a powerful impact on mothers who came here to remember their fallen sons.

A solemn silence and a stony chill fill the basilica. At 300  yards long, the basilica was built to be longer than St. Peter's...but the Vatican had the final say when it blessed only 262 of those yards. Many Spaniards pass under the huge, foreboding angels of fascism to visit the grave of General Franco—an unusual place of pilgrimage, to say the least.

After walking through the two long vestibules, stop at the iron gates of the actual basilica. The line of torch-like lamps adds to the shrine ambience. Franco's prisoners, the enemies of the right, dug this memorial out of solid rock from 1940 to 1950. (Though it looks like bare rock still shows on the ceiling, it's just a clever design.) The sides of the monument are lined with copies of 16th-century Brussels tapestries of the Apocalypse, and side chapels contain alabaster copies of Spain's most famous statues of the Virgin Mary.

Interred behind the high altar and side chapels (marked "RIP, 1936–1939, died for God and country") are the remains of the approximately 50,000 people, both Franco's Nationalists and the anti-Franco Republicans, who lost their lives in the war. Regrettably, the urns are not visible, so it is Franco who takes center stage. His grave, strewn with flowers, lies behind the high altar. In front of the altar is the grave of José Antonio Primo de Rivera (1903–1936), the founder of Spanish fascism, who was killed by Republicans during the Civil War. Between these fascists' graves, the statue of a crucified Christ is lashed to a timber Franco himself is said to have felled. The seeping stones seem to weep for the victims. Today, families of the buried Republicans remain upset that their kin are lying with Franco and his Nationalists.

As you leave, stare into the eyes of those angels with swords and two right wings and think about all the "heroes" who keep dying "for God and country," at the request of the latter. A Mass closes off the entire front of the basilica (altar and tombs) to the public daily from 11:00 to 12:05. The resident boys' choir (the

"White Voices"—Spain's answer to the Vienna Boys' Choir) generally sings during the Mass (you can sit through the service, but not sightsee during this time).

The expansive view from the monument's terrace includes the peaceful, forested valley and sometimes snow-streaked mountains. For an even better view, consider taking a **funicular** trip—with a short commentary in English—to the base of the cross (€1.50 one-way, €2.50 round-trip, pay fare at machine, April–Sept Tue–Sun 11:00–18:30, 3/hr; Oct–March Tue–Sun 11:00–16:30, 2/hr; closed Mon, last ticket sold 30 min before closing; restaurant and public WC). You can hike back down in 25 minutes. If you have a car, you can drive up past the monastery and hike from the start of the trail marked *Sendero a la Cruz*.

Sleeping and Eating: Near the parking lot and bus stop at Valley of the Fallen are a small snack bar and picnic tables. Basic overnight lodging is available at the **Hospedería del Valle de los Caídos,** a 100-room monastery behind the cross (Sb-€46, Db-€91, includes meals, tax, and a pass to enter and leave the park after hours, tel. 918-905-494, fax 918-961-542, no English spoken). A meditative night here is good mostly for monks.

Segovia

Fifty miles from Madrid, this town of 55,000 boasts a thrilling Roman aqueduct, a grand cathedral, and a historic castle. Since the city is more than 3,000 feet above sea level and just northwest of a mountain range, the city is exposed to cool northern breezes, and people come here from Madrid for a break from the summer heat.

Day-Tripping from Madrid: Considering the easy train and bus connections (35 min one-way by AVE train, 2 hours by slower train, 1.5 hours by bus), Segovia makes a fine day trip from Madrid. The disadvantages of side-tripping are that you spend the coolest hours of the day (early and late) en route, you miss the charming evening scene in Segovia, and you'll pay more for a hotel in Madrid than in Segovia. If you have time, spend the night. But even if you just stay the day, Segovia still offers a rewarding and convenient break from the big-city intensity of Madrid.

Orientation to Segovia

Segovia is a medieval "ship" ready for your inspection. Start at the stern—the aqueduct—and stroll up Calle de Cervantes and Calle Juan Bravo to the prickly Gothic masts of the cathedral. Explore the tangle of narrow streets around playful Plaza Mayor and then descend to the Alcázar at the bow.

Tourist Information

Segovia has four TIs. The TI on Plaza Mayor covers both Segovia and the surrounding region (at #10, July–mid-Sept daily 9:00–20:00, mid-Sept–June 9:00–14:00 & 16:00–19:00, tel. 921-460-334). The TI at Plaza del Azoguejo at the base of the aqueduct specializes in Segovia and has lots of friendly staff, WCs, and a gift shop (daily 10:00–19:00, Sat until 20:00, see wooden model of Segovia, tel. 921-466-720, www.segovia.es). Two smaller TIs are at the bus station (behind a window, daily 10:00–14:00 & 15:30–17:00) and at the AVE train station (Mon–Fri 9:00–17:00, Sat–Sun 10:30–18:30, tel. 921-447-262).

Arrival in Segovia

Unfortunately, neither of the train stations nor the bus station has luggage storage. If day-tripping from Madrid, check the return schedule when you arrive here (or get one at the Segovia TI).

By Bus: It's a 10-minute walk from the bus station to the town center: Exit left out of the station, continue straight across the street, and follow Avenida Fernández Ladreda, passing San Millán church on the left, then San Clemente church on the right, before coming to the aqueduct.

By Train: From the **AVE train station** (called Guiomar), ride bus #11 for 20 minutes to the base of the aqueduct. To reach the center from the less-convenient *Cercanías* **train station,** you can catch bus #6 or #8; take a taxi; or walk 35 minutes (start at Paseo del Conde de Sepulvedana—which becomes Paseo Ezequiel González—to the bus station, then turn right and head down Avenida Fernández Ladreda to the aqueduct).

By Car: See "Route Tips for Drivers," page 103.

Helpful Hints

Shopping: If you buy handicrafts such as tablecloths from street vendors, make sure the item you're buying is the one you actually get; some unscrupulous vendors substitute inferior goods at the last minute. A flea market is held on Plaza Mayor on Thursdays (roughly 8:00–15:00).

Local Guide: Elvira Valderrama Rascon, a hardworking young woman, is a good English-speaking guide (€100/half-day tour, mobile 636-227-949, elvisvalrras@yahoo.es).

Sightseeing Bus: Bus Turístico is a weak version of a hop-on, hop-off bus, but it does give you a nice chance to take great panoramic photos of Segovia's boat-like shape, with the mountains as a backdrop. Pick it up at the aqueduct, and stay on—it's not really worth using it as a means of getting around town; just stay on for the full loop (€5.60, buy ticket on bus; leaves at 11:00, 12:00, 13:00, 16:00, and 17:00; tel. 902-330-080).

Self-Guided Walk

Welcome to Historic Segovia

This 15-minute walk is all downhill from the city's main square along the pedestrian-only street to the Roman aqueduct. It's most enjoyable just before dinner, when it's cool and filled with strolling locals.

Start on Segovia's inviting **Plaza Mayor**—once the scene of executions, religious theater, and bullfights with spectators jam-

ming the balconies. In the 19th century, the bullfights were stopped. When locals complained, they were given a more gentle form of entertainment—bands in the music kiosk. Today the very best entertainment here is simply enjoying a light meal, snack, or drink in your choice of the many restaurants and cafés lining the square. The Renaissance church opposite the City Hall and behind the TI was built to replace the church where Isabel was proclaimed Queen of Castile in 1474. The symbol of Segovia is the aqueduct—find it in the seals on the Theater Juan Bravo and atop the City Hall. Head down Calle de Isabel la Católica (downhill, to right of Hotel Infanta Isabel), and tempt yourself with the pastries in the window display of the corner bakery.

After 100 yards, at the first intersection, you'll see the Corpus Christi Convent on the right. For a donation, you can pop in to see the Franciscan church, which was once a synagogue, which was once a mosque. While sweet and peaceful, with lots of art featuring St. Francis, the church is skippable.

After another 100 yards, you come to the complicated Plaza de San Martín, a commotion of history surrounding a striking statue of Juan Bravo. When Charles V, a Habsburg who didn't even speak Spanish, took power, he imposed his rule over Castile. This threatened the local nobles, who—inspired and led by Juan

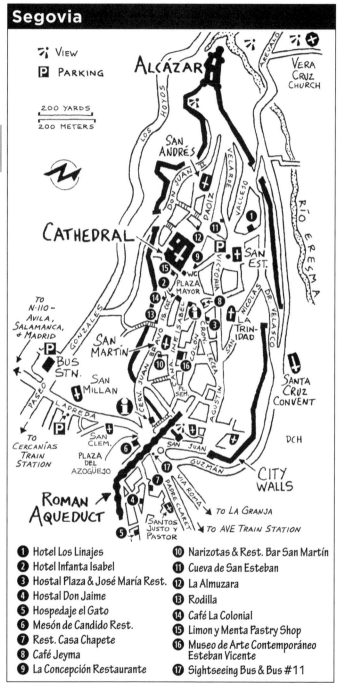

Segovia

VIEW

P PARKING

200 YARDS
200 METERS

ALCÁZAR

VERA CRUZ CHURCH

REVALO

LOS HOYOS

SAN ANDRÉS

DON JUAN

VELARDE

VALLEJO

DAOIZ

RÍO ERESMA

CATHEDRAL

1

11

12

P

SAN EST.

9

15

WC

2 PLAZA MAYOR

VICTORIA

14

8

13 IS. CAT.

3

LA TRINIDAD

NICOLÁS

DR. VELASCO

GONZALES

SAN MARTÍN

INF. ISABEL

CERV. JUAN BRAVO

COLÓN

CRON. LECEA

SAN AGUSTÍN

TO N-110 – AVILA, SALAMANCA, & MADRID

P

BUS STN.

SAN MILLAN

10

16

PL. SEM.

PASEO

LA PREDA

P

SAN CLEM.

6

SAN JUAN

17

TO CERCANÍAS TRAIN STATION

PLAZA DEL AZOGÜEJO

7

PADRE CLARET

VIA ROMA

GUZMÁN

TO LA GRANJA

TO AVE TRAIN STATION

CITY WALLS

SANTA CRUZ CONVENT

DCH

ROMAN AQUEDUCT

4

5

SANTOS JUSTO Y PASTOR

1 Hotel Los Linajes
2 Hotel Infanta Isabel
3 Hostal Plaza & José María Rest.
4 Hostal Don Jaime
5 Hospedaje el Gato
6 Mesón de Candido Rest.
7 Rest. Casa Chapete
8 Café Jeyma
9 La Concepción Restaurante

10 Narizotas & Rest. Bar San Martín
11 Cueva de San Esteban
12 La Almuzara
13 Rodilla
14 Café La Colonial
15 Limon y Menta Pastry Shop
16 Museo de Arte Contemporáneo Esteban Vicente
17 Sightseeing Bus & Bus #11

Bravo—revolted in 1521. Although Juan Bravo lost the battle—and his head—he's still a symbol of Castilian pride. This statue was erected in 1921 on the 400th anniversary of his death.

On the same square, the 12th-century Church of St. Martín is Segovian Romanesque in style (a mix of Christian Romanesque and Moorish styles). The 14th-century Tower of Lozoya, behind the statue, is one of many fortified towers that marked the homes of feuding local noble families. Clashing loyalties led to mini–civil wars. In the 15th century, as Ferdinand and Isabel centralized authority in Spain, nobles were required to lop their towers. You'll see the once-tall, now-stubby towers of 15th-century noble mansions all over Segovia.

In front of the Juan Bravo statue (downhill end of square) stands the bold and bulky House of Siglo XV. Its fortified *Isabelino* style was typical of 15th-century Segovian houses. Later, in a more peaceful age, the boldness of these houses was softened with the decorative stucco work—Arabic-style floral and geometrical patterns—that you see today (for example, in the big house across the street). At Plaza del Platero Oquendo, 50 yards farther downhill on the right, you'll see a similar once-fortified, now-softened house with a cropped tower.

At the next corner, find the "house of a thousand beaks" with another truncated tower. This building, maintaining its original Moorish design, has a wall just past the door, which blocks your view from the street. This wall, the architectural equivalent of a veil, hid this home's fine courtyard—Moors didn't flaunt their wealth. Step inside; there may be art students at work and perhaps an exhibit on display.

From here, stroll 100 yards, and you'll see the Roman aqueduct, which marks the end of this walk (and is described next).

Sights

▲**Roman Aqueduct**—Segovia was a Roman military base and needed water. Emperor Trajan's engineers built a nine-mile aque-

duct to channel water from the Río Frío to the city, culminating at the Roman castle (which is the Alcázar today). The famous and exposed section of the 2,000-year-old *acueducto romano* is 2,500 feet long and 100 feet high, has 118 arches, was made from 20,000 granite blocks without any mortar, and can still carry a stream of water. It actually functioned until the late 19th century. On Plaza del Azoguejo, a grand

NORTHWEST OF MADRID

stairway leads from the base of the aqueduct to the top—offering close-up looks at the imposing work.

▲**Cathedral**—Segovia's cathedral, built in Renaissance times

(1525–1768, the third on this site), was Spain's last major Gothic building. Embellished to the hilt with pinnacles and flying buttresses, the exterior is a great example of the final, overripe stage of Gothic, called Flamboyant. Yet the Renaissance arrived before it was finished—as evidenced by the fact that the cathedral is crowned by a dome, not a spire.

Cost and Hours: €3, free on Sun 9:30–13:15 but cathedral access only—no cloisters, open daily April–Oct 9:30–18:30, Nov–March 9:00–17:30, tel. 921-462-205.

⊘ Self-Guided Tour: The spacious and elegantly simple interior provides a delightful contrast to the frilly exterior. The **choir** features finely carved wooden stalls from the previous church (1400s). The *catedra* (bishop's chair) is in the center rear of the choir. The many side chapels are mostly 16th-century, and come with big locking gates—a reminder that they were the private sacred domain of the rich families and guilds who "owned" them. They could enjoy private Masses here with their names actually spoken in the blessings, and a fine burial spot close to the altar. Find the **Capilla La Concepción** (a chapel in the rear that looks like a mini art gallery). Its many 17th-century paintings hang behind a mahogany wood gate imported from colonial America. The painting *Tree of Life*, by Ignacio Ries (left of the altar), shows hedonistic mortals dancing atop the Tree of Life. As a skeletal Grim Reaper

prepares to receive them into hell (by literally chopping down the tree... timberrrr), Jesus rings a bell imploring them to wake up before it's too late. The center statue is Mary of the Apocalypse (as described in Revelations, standing on a devil and half moon, which looks like bull's horns). Mary's pregnant and the devil licks his evil chops, waiting to devour the baby Messiah.

Opposite from where you entered, a fine door (which leads into the cloister) is crowned by a painted Flamboyant Gothic *pietà* in its tympanum (the statue of Jesus with a skirt, on the left, is a reminder of how prudishness from the past looks silly in the present).

The **cloisters** hold a fine little one-room museum containing French tapestries, paintings, and silver reliquaries. Outside in the courtyard, a glass case holds keys to the 17th-century private-chapel gates. The gilded chapter room is draped with precious Flemish tapestries. Notice the gilded wagon. The Holy Communion wafer is placed in the top of this temple-like cart and paraded through town each year during the Corpus Christi festival. From the cloister courtyard, you can see the Renaissance dome rising above the otherwise Gothic rooftop.

▲**Alcázar**—In the Middle Ages, this fortified palace was one of the favorite residences of the monarchs of Castile, a key fortress for controlling the region. The Alcázar grew through the ages, and its function changed many times: After its stint as a palace, it was a prison for 200 years, and then a Royal Artillery School. It burned in 1862. Since the fire, it's basically been a museum.

Cost and Hours: €4 for palace, €2 for tower, daily April–Sept 10:00–19:00, Oct–March 10:00–18:00 (tower closed third Tue of month). Buy your tickets at Real Laboratorio de Chimia, facing the palace on your left. At the entrance, pass your ticket through the turnstiles on the right for the palace, or the turnstiles on the left for the tower. The 45-minute €3 audioguide describes each room. Pick up a free English leaflet. Tel. 921-460-759.

❸ **Self-Guided Tour:** You'll enjoy a one-way route through 11 rooms, including a fine view terrace. Visit the tower afterward (€2); its 152 steps up a tight spiral staircase reward you with the only 360-degree city view in town. What you see today in the Alcázar is rebuilt—a Disney-esque exaggeration of the original. Still, its fine Moorish decor and historic furnishings are fascinating. The sumptuous ceilings are accurately restored in Mudejar style, and the throne-room ceiling is the artistic highlight of the palace.

You'll see a big **mural** of Queen Isabel the Catholic being proclaimed Queen of Castile and León in Segovia's main square in 1474. The Hall of the Monarchs is lined with the busts of the 52 rulers of Castile and León who ruled during the long and ultimately successful Reconquista (711–1492): from Pelayo (the first), clockwise to Juana VII (the last). There were only seven queens during the period (the numbered ones). In this current age of Islamic extremists decapitating Christians, study the painting of St. James the Moor-Slayer—with Muslim heads literally rolling at his feet (poignantly...in the chapel). James is the patron saint of Spain. His name was the rallying cry in the centuries-long Christian crusade to push the Muslim Moors back into Africa.

Stepping onto the **terrace** (the site of the original Roman military camp, circa A.D. 100) with its vast views, marvel at the natural fortification provided by this promontory cut by the confluence of two rivers. The terrace is closed in the winter and sometimes on windy days. The Alcázar marks the end (and physical low point) of the gradual downhill course of the nine-mile-long Roman aqueduct. Can you find the mountain nicknamed *Mujer Muerta* ("dead woman")?

In the **armory** (just after the terrace), find the king's 16th-century ornately carved ivory crossbow, with the hunting scene shown in the adjacent painting. The final rooms are the Museum of Artillery, recalling the period (1764–1862) when this was the Royal Artillery School. It shows the evolution of explosive weaponry, with old photos and prints of the Alcázar.

Church of Santos Justo y Pastor—This simple yet stately old church has fascinating 12th- and 13th-century frescoes filled with Gothic symbolism, plus a stork's nest atop its tower. From the base of the aqueduct, it's a short climb uphill into the newer part of town (free, Tue–Sat 11:00–14:00 & 16:00–18:00; closed Sun–Mon and when the volunteer caretaker, Rafael, needs to run an errand; located a couple of blocks from Plaza del Azoguejo). Kind old Rafael probably won't let you risk climbing the dangerous, claustrophobic bell tower for a commanding Segovia view until they've finished cleaning the pigeon poop and renovating the tower, which may take a while, as they're having trouble gathering sufficient resources to finish the job.

Museo de Arte Contemporáneo Esteban Vicente—A collection of local artist Esteban Vicente's abstract art is housed in two rooms of the remodeled remains of Henry IV's 1455 palace. Wilder than Rothko but more restrained than Pollock, his vibrant work influenced post-WWII American art. The temporary exhibits can be more interesting than the permanent collection (€3, free on Thu, roughly Tue–Fri 11:00–14:00 & 16:00–19:00, Sat–Sun 11:00–20:00, closed Mon, tel. 921-426-010).

Near Segovia

Vera Cruz Church—This 12-sided, 13th-century Romanesque church, built by the Knights Templar, once housed a piece of the "true cross" (€2, Tue–Sun 10:30–13:30 & 15:30–19:00, closed Mon and Nov, closes at 18:00 in winter, outside town beyond the castle, a 25-min walk from main square, tel. 921-431-475). There's a postcard view of the city from here, and more views follow as you continue around Segovia on the small road below the castle, labeled *ruta turística panorámica*.

▲**La Granja Palace**—This "little Versailles," six miles south of Segovia, is much smaller and happier than nearby El Escorial. The palace and gardens were built by the homesick French-born King Philip V, grandson of Louis XIV. Today, it's restored to its original

18th-century splendor, with its royal collection of tapestries, clocks, and crystal (actually made at the palace's royal crystal factory). Plumbers and gardeners imported from France and Italy made Philip a garden that rivaled Versailles'. The fanciful fountains feature mythological stories (explained in the palace audioguide). The Bourbon Philip chose to be buried here rather than with his Habsburg predecessors at El Escorial. His tomb is in the adjacent church, included with your ticket (€5 with Spanish-speaking guide, €4.50 without guide, April–Sept Tue–Sun 10:00–18:00, closed Mon; Oct–March Tue–Sat 10:00–13:30 & 15:00–17:00, Sun 10:00–14:00, closed Mon; tel. 921-470-019, www.patrimonionacional .es). Fourteen buses a day (fewer on weekends) make the 25-minute trip from Segovia (catch at the bus station) to San Ildefonso–La Granja. The park is free (daily 10:00–20:00, until 19:00 in winter).

Sleeping in Segovia

The best places are on or near the central Plaza Mayor. This is where the city action is: the best bars, most touristic and *típico* eateries, and the TI. During busy times—on weekends and in July and August—arrive early or call ahead.

In the Old Center, near Plaza Mayor

$$$ Hotel Los Linajes is ultra-classy, with rusticity mixed into its newly poured concrete. This poor man's parador is a few blocks beyond Plaza Mayor, with territorial views and modern, air-conditioned niceties (Sb-€81, Db-€110, big Db-€142, Tb-€131, cheaper off-season, breakfast-€10, elevator, parking-€13, Dr. Velasco 9, tel. 921-460-475, fax 921-460-479, www.loslinajes.com, hotellos linajes@terra.es). From Plaza Mayor, take Escuderos downhill; at the five-way intersection, angle right on Dr. Velasco. Drivers, follow brown hotel signs from the aqueduct to its tight but handy garage.

$$$ Hotel Infanta Isabel, right on Plaza Mayor, is the ritziest hotel in the old town, with 38 elegant rooms, some with plaza views (Sb-€67–77, Db-€97–114 depending on room size, less in winter, breakfast on the square-€9, elevator, valet parking-€12, tel. 921-461-300, fax 921-462-217, www.hotelinfantaisabel.com, admin@hotelinfantaisabel.com).

$$ Hostal Plaza, just off Plaza Mayor, has extremely strict management, snaky corridors, and some tight squeezes. But its

Sleep Code

(€1 = about $1.40, country code: 34)
S = Single, **D** = Double/Twin, **T** = Triple, **Q** = Quad, **b** = bathroom, **s** = shower only. Unless otherwise noted, you can assume credit cards are accepted and English is spoken. Breakfast is generally not included.

To help you easily sort through these listings, I've divided the rooms into three categories, based on the price for a standard double room with bath during high season (breakfast not included):

$$$ Higher Priced—Most rooms €85 or more.
$$ Moderately Priced—Most rooms between €30-85.
$ Lower Priced—Most rooms €30 or less.

28 rooms are clean and cozy (Sb-€39, D-€35, Db-€48, Tb-€65, breakfast-€2.50, parking-€10, Cronista Lecea 11, tel. 921-460-303, fax 921-460-305, www.hostal-plaza.com, informacion@hostal -plaza.com).

Outside of the Old Town, near the Aqueduct

$$ Hostal Don Jaime, opposite the Church of San Justo, is a friendly family-run place with 38 basic, worn yet well-maintained rooms. Seven more rooms are in an annex across the street (S-€25, D-€32, Db-€50, Tb-€60, Qb-€70, show this book and get a free breakfast in 2010—otherwise €3.50, parking-€8, Ochoa Ondategui 8; from TI at Plaza del Azogüejo, cross under the aqueduct, go right, angle left, then snake uphill for 2 blocks; tel. & fax 921-444- 787, hostaldonjaime@hotmail.com).

$$ Hospedaje el Gato, a family-run place on a quiet nondescript square just outside the old town, has 10 modern, comfortable rooms (Sb-€25, Db-€40, Tb-€55, air-con, smoky bar serves breakfast and good tapas, parking-€10, uphill from Hostal Don Jaime and aqueduct at Plaza del Salvador 10, tel. 921-423-244, mobile 678-405-079, fax 921-438-047, hbarelgato@yahoo.es but prefer phone or fax reservations).

Eating in Segovia

Look for Segovia's culinary claim to fame, roast suckling pig (*cochinillo asado:* 21 days of mother's milk, into the oven, and onto your plate—oh, Babe). It's worth a splurge here, or in Toledo or Salamanca.

For lighter fare, try *sopa castellana*—soup mixed with eggs, ham, garlic, and bread—or warm yourself up with the local *judiones de La Granja*, a popular soup made with flat white beans from the region.

Ponche segoviano, a dessert made with an almond-and-honey *mazapán* base, is heavenly after an earthy dinner or with a coffee in the afternoon (at the recommended Limon y Menta, described on the next page).

Roast Suckling Pig

Mesón de Cándido, one of the top restaurants in Castile, is famous for its memorable dinners. Even though it's filled with tourists, it's a grand experience. Take time to wander around and survey the photos of celebs—from King Juan Carlos to Antonio Banderas and Melanie Griffith—who've suckled here. Try to get a table in a room with an aqueduct view (figure on spending €35–40, daily 13:00–16:30 & 20:00–23:00, Plaza del Azogüejo 5, air-con, under aqueduct, call 921-428-103 for reservations, www.mesonde candido.es, candido@mesondecandido.es). Three gracious generations of the Cándido family still run the show.

José María is *the* place to pig out in the old town, a block off Plaza Mayor. While it doesn't have the history or fanfare of Cándido, locals claim this high-energy place serves the best roast suckling pig in town. It thrives with a hungry mix of tourists and locals—so reservations are usually necessary (€40 à la carte dinner, daily 13:00–16:00 & 20:30–23:30, air-con, Cronista Lecea 11, tel. 921-466-017, reservas@rtejosemaria.com).

Restaurante Casa Chapete, a homey little place filled with smoke, happy locals, and not a tourist in sight, serves traditional lamb and pig dishes—but only for lunch (€22 three-course meals including wine, €35 quarter *cochinillos* for 2–3 people, €9 simple three-course fixed-price meals on weekdays, daily 12:30–16:00, 2 blocks beyond aqueduct, across from recommended Hostal Don Jaime at Calle Ochoa Ondategui 7, tel. 921-421-096).

The Old Center (No Pig)

Plaza Mayor, the main square, provides a great backdrop for a light lunch, dinner, or drink. Prices at the cafés are generally reasonable, and many offer a good selection of tapas and *raciones*. Grab a table at the place of your choice and savor the scene. **Café Jeyma** has a fine setting and cathedral view. **La Concepción Restaurante** is also good (€35 meals, closer to the cathedral).

Narizotas serves more imaginative and non-Castilian alternatives to the gamey traditions. You'll dine outside on a delightful square or inside with modern art under medieval timbers. For a wonderful dining experience, try their chef's choice mystery samplers, either the "Right Hand" (€37, about 10 courses, with wine and dessert) or the "Left Hand" (€33, about six courses, with wine and dessert). They offer a less elaborate three-course €16 fixed-priced meal, and their à la carte menu is also a treat (daily 13:00–16:00 & 20:30–24:00, midway down Calle Juan Bravo at Plaza de Medina del Campo 1, tel. 921-462-679).

Restaurante Bar San Martín, a no-frills place popular with locals, has a lively tapas bar, great outdoor seating by a fountain on the same square as the recommended Narizotas, and a smoky restaurant in the back. I'd eat here only to enjoy the setting on the square (€10 three-course fixed-price meal on weekdays, tapas bar open Tue–Sun 9:00–24:00, restaurant open Tue–Sun 13:30–16:00 & 20:30–23:00, both closed Mon, Plaza de San Martín 3, tel. 921-462-466).

Cueva de San Esteban serves traditional home cooking with a stress-free photo menu at the door, and hearty, big-enough-to-split plates (daily 11:00–24:00, full meals 13:00–16:00, two blocks past Plaza Mayor on a quiet back street, Calle Valdelaguila 15, tel. 921-460-982).

La Almuzara is a garden of veggie and organic delights: whole-wheat pizzas, tofu, seitan, and even a few dishes with meat (€10 plates, Tue 20:00–24:00, Wed–Sun 13:00–16:00 & 20:00–24:00, closed Mon, between cathedral and Alcázar at Marques del Arco 3, tel. 921-460-622).

Rodilla, the popular chain, offers a tasty selection of sand-wiches and salads (Mon–Fri 9:30–22:00, Sat–Sun 10:00–22:30, on Calle Juan Bravo, at intersection with Calle de la Herrería).

Breakfast: For breakfast, I like to sit on Plaza Mayor enjoying the cool air and the people scene (many choices). Or, 100 yards down the main drag toward the aqueduct, **Café La Colonial** serves good breakfasts (with seating on a tiny square or inside, Plaza del Corpus).

Nightlife: Inexpensive bars and eateries line Calle de Infanta Isabel, just off Plaza Mayor. For nightlife, the bars on Plaza Mayor, Calle de Infanta Isabel, and Calle Isabel la Católica are packed. There are a number of late-night dance clubs along the aqueduct.

Dessert: **Limon y Menta** offers a good, rich *ponche segoviano* (marzipan) cake by the slice for €3, or try the lighter honey-and-almond *crocantinos* (daily 9:30–21:30 but hours can vary, seating inside, Isabel La Católica 2, tel. 921-462-141).

Market: An outdoor produce market thrives on Plaza Mayor on Thursday (roughly 8:00–15:00). Nearby, a few stalls are open daily except Sunday on Calle del Cronista Ildefonso Rodríguez.

Connections

If you're side-tripping between Segovia and Madrid, note that the 35-minute AVE train takes less than half as long as the bus. However, you'll spend more time getting to the AVE Stations in Segovia and Madrid than to the bus stations, so the total time spent in transit is about the same. (In Madrid, the AVE goes to the Chamartín train station, while the bus goes to Príncipe Pío Metro station.) *Cercanías* commuter trains also run to Madrid, but take two hours and don't save you much money.

From Segovia by Bus to: La Granja Palace (14/day, fewer on weekends, 25 min), **Ávila** (5/day weekdays, 2/day weekends, 1 hr), **Madrid** (2/hr, departing on the half-hour, 1.25 hrs, €7; Mon–Sat first departure at 6:30, last return at 21:30; Sun first at 8:30, last at 22:30; many stop first at Madrid's Metro: Moncloa, where you can get off if convenient to your hotel, and the end of the line is the Príncipe Pío bus terminal and Metro stop, tel. 915-598-955, www .lasepulvedana.es), **Salamanca** (2/day, 3 hrs, transfer in Labajos; it's smart to call ahead to reserve a seat for the Labajos–Salamanca segment—call Madrid's La Sepulvedana office at tel. 915-598-955 to book your seat). Consider busing from Segovia to Ávila for a visit, then continuing to Salamanca by bus or train.

If you're riding the bus from Madrid to Segovia, about 30 minutes after leaving Madrid you'll see—breaking the horizon on the left—the dramatic concrete cross of the Valley of the Fallen. Its grand facade marks the entry to the mammoth underground memorial (described earlier in this chapter).

By Train to: Madrid (via high-speed AVE train: 8/day, 35 min, €10, leaves from Segovia's Guiomar Station, arrives at Madrid's Chamartín Station; via *cercanías* commuter train: 9/day, 2 hrs, €6, leaves from Segovia's inconvenient *Cercanías* Station, arrives in Madrid at both Chamartín and Atocha Stations). AVE trains leave from Segovia's Guiomar Station; to get there, take city bus #11 from the base of the aqueduct (20 min, buses usually timed to match arrivals). To reach the sleepy, dead-end *Cercanías* Station, walk 20 minutes past the bus station along Paseo de Ezequiel González (which turns into Paseo del Conde de Sepulvedana); catch bus #6 (leaves from the bus station) or #8 (leaves from the aqueduct); or take a taxi. Train info: tel. 902-240-202.

Route Tips for Drivers
From Madrid to Segovia: Leave Madrid on A-6. Exit 39 gets you to Segovia via a slow, winding route over the scenic mountain. Exit at 60 (after a long €3 toll tunnel) or get there quicker by staying on the toll road all the way to Segovia (add €2 weekdays or €3 on weekends). At the Segovia aqueduct, follow *casco histórico* signs to

the old town (on the side where the aqueduct adjoins the crenellated fortress walls).

Parking in Segovia: Free parking is available in the Alcázar's lot, but you must move your car out by 19:00 (or by 18:00 Oct–March), when the gates close. Or try the lot northwest of the bus station by the statue of Cándido, along the street called Paseo de Ezequiel González. Outside the old city, there's an Acueducto Parking underground garage kitty-corner from the bus station. Although it can be a hard slog up the hill to the Alcázar on a hot day, it beats trying to maneuver uphill through tight bends. A huge garage is planned near the aqueduct (possibly completed in time for your visit).

While the city center has lots of parking spaces, they're not free. If you want to park in the old town, be legal or risk an expensive ticket. Buy a ticket from the nearby machine to park in areas marked by blue stripes, and place the ticket on your dashboard (€1.40/hr, pay meter every 2 hours 9:00–14:00 & 16:30–20:00; free parking 20:00–9:00, Sat afternoon, and all day Sun).

Segovia to Salamanca (100 miles): Leave Segovia by driving around the town's circular road, which offers good views from below the Alcázar. Then follow signs for *Ávila* (road N-110). Notice the fine Segovia view from the three crosses at the crest of the first hill. The Salamanca road leads around the famous Ávila walls to the right. The best wall view is from the signposted Cuatro Postes, a mile northwest of town. Salamanca (N-501) is clearly marked, about an hour's drive away.

About 20 miles before Salamanca, you might want to stop at the huge bull on the left side of the road. There's a little dirt lane leading right up to it. As you get closer, it becomes more and more obvious it isn't real. Bad boys climb it for a goofy photo. For a great photo op of Salamanca, complete with river reflection, stop at the edge of the city (at the light before the first bridge). In Salamanca, the only safe parking is in a garage; try the underground lot at Plaza Santa Eulalia, Plaza del  Campillo, or Lemans (closer to recommended Petit Palace Las Torres), or even easier, try one of the hotels with valet parking for comparable fees. See the Salamanca chapter for more information.

Ávila

Yet another popular side-trip from Madrid, Ávila is famous for its perfectly preserved medieval walls, as the birthplace of St. Teresa, and for its yummy *yema* treats. For more than 300 years, Ávila was on the battlefront between the Muslims and Christians, changing hands several times. Today, perfectly peaceful Ávila has a charming old town. With several fine churches and monasteries, it makes for an enjoyable quick stop between Segovia and Salamanca (each about an hour away by car).

Orientation to Ávila

On a quick stop, everything in Ávila that matters is within a few blocks of the cathedral (actually part of the east end of the wall).

Tourist Information

The TI has fine, free maps and information on walking tours (daily 9:30–14:00 & 16:00–19:00, no afternoon closure July–mid-Sept, on Calle San Segundo, just outside the wall gate near the cathedral, tel. 920-211-387). Another TI, with a friendlier staff, is located outside the wall, opposite the Basilica of San Vicente (daily April–Oct 10:00–20:00, Nov–March 10:00–18:00, public WCs).

Sightseeing Train: A clunky tourist train departs from outside the wall by Puerta de San Vicente, heads into town, exits at the westernmost gate, loops by the Monasterio de la Encarnación (where St. Teresa lived), and then shudders along back to the north wall. Unfortunately, its daytime route doesn't stop at the worthwhile Cuatro Postes viewpoint (though it does stop there for a view of the illuminated wall at 22:00 on Fri–Sat in July–Aug). Check the *próxima salida* sign for departure times, which are usually twice an hour (€4 day, €7 night, daily 9:00–18:00, narration in Spanish unless you specify English, mobile 629-222-218).

Arrival in Ávila

Approaching by bus, train, or car, you'll need to make your way through the nondescript modern part of town to find the walled old town. From the cathedral and wall, the bus station is a 15-minute walk, while the train station is a 20-minute walk. City buses #4 and #1 run from the train station to the Basilica of San Vicente (to find the bus stop, exit the station to the right and walk one block). There are lockers at Ávila's bus station (use the newer-looking locks), but not at the train station. Drivers can use the public parking east of Puerta del Alcázar, just south of the cathedral, or at Parking Dornier (€1.25/hour).

NORTHWEST OF MADRID

Sights in Ávila

▲**The Wall**—Built from around 1100 on even more ancient remains, Ávila's fortified wall is the oldest, most complete, and best-preserved in Spain. It has four entrances, allowing visitors the chance to walk almost three-quarters of the wall: One entrance is just off Plaza de Santa Teresa (Puerta del Alcázar). The best one, which leads to a longer walk, starts at the gate closest to the cathedral (Puerta del Peso de la Harina) and takes you to the third, Puerta del Carmen (look for the door marked *subida a la muralla*). The fourth is at Puerta Puente Adaja, on the end farthest from the cathedral, and leads to only a small section of the wall (€4, April–mid-Oct Tue–Sun 10:00–20:00, mid-Oct–March 11:00–18:00, closed Mon except July–Aug, last entry 30 min before closing). A night visit gives you the same walk, with the wall beautifully lit (€4, mid-June–mid-Sept Sun–Wed 22:00–24:00). Your ticket has multiple stubs, which allow you to enter the wall at various points. You can use one stub to go up during the day, and save another to go up at night.

There's an interesting paseo scene along the wall each night—make your way along the southern wall (Paseo del Rastro) to Plaza de Santa Teresa for spectacular vistas across the plains. The best views of the wall itself are actually from street level (especially along the north side, which drivers will see as they circle to the right from Puerta de San Vicente to catch the highway to Salamanca). The finest overall view of the walled town is about a mile away on the Salamanca road (N-501), at a clearly marked turnout for the Cuatro Postes (four posts).

Cathedral—While it started as Romanesque, Ávila's cathedral, finished in the 16th century, is considered the first Gothic cathedral in Spain. Its position—with its granite apse actually part of the fortified wall—underlines the "medieval alliance between cross and sword." For €4, you can tour the cathedral, its sacristy, cloister, and museum—which includes an El Greco painting (Mon–Sat 10:00–19:30, Sun 12:00–17:00, off-season Mon–Sat 10:00–17:00, Sun 12:00–17:00—but hours often vary, Plaza de la Catedral).

Convent of St. Teresa—Built in the 17th century on the spot where the saint was born, this convent is a big hit with pilgrims (10-min walk from cathedral). A lavishly gilded side chapel marks the actual place of her birth (left of main altar, door may be closed). A separate room of relics (outside, facing the church on your right,

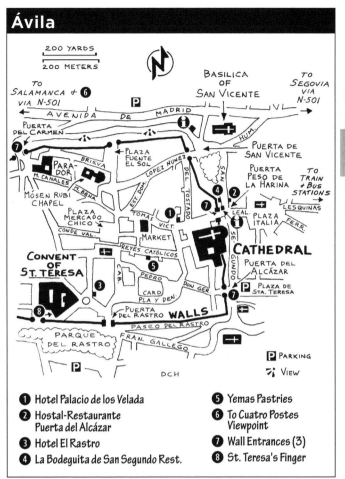

Ávila

200 YARDS
200 METERS

TO
SALAMANCA & 6
VIA N-501

BASILICA
OF
SAN VICENTE

TO
SEGOVIA
VIA
N-501

AVENIDA   DE   MADRID

PUERTA
DEL CARMEN

PUERTA DE
SAN VICENTE

PLAZA
FUENTE
EL SOL

PARA-
DOR

M. CANALES   BRIEVA

EL BENA

PUERTA
PESO DE
LA HARINA

TO
TRAIN
& BUS
STATIONS

LES QUINAS

MÓSEN RUBÍ
CHAPEL

PLAZA
MERCADO
CHICO

LOPEZ NUÑEZ

EST. DOM.

DEL TOSTADO

SAN

LEAL.

PLAZA
ITALIA

FERR.

CONDE VAL.

TOMÁS

VICT.

MARKET

CONVENT
OF
ST. TERESA

REYES CATÓLICOS

PEPRO

CAB.

CARD.
PLA Y DEN.

DON GER.

SE GUNDO

CATHEDRAL

PUERTA DEL
ALCÁZAR

PLAZA DE
STA. TERESA

PUERTA
DEL RASTRO

WALLS

PASEO DEL RASTRO

PARQUE
DEL RASTRO

FRAN. GALLEGO

P PARKING

VIEW

DCH

1 Hotel Palacio de los Velada

2 Hostal-Restaurante
   Puerta del Alcázar

3 Hotel El Rastro

4 La Bodeguita de San Segundo Rest.

5 Yemas Pastries

6 To Cuatro Postes
   Viewpoint

7 Wall Entrances (3)

8 St. Teresa's Finger

Sala de Reliquias) houses a shop that shows off Teresa's finger, complete with a fancy emerald ring, along with one of her sandals and the bones of St. John of the Cross (free, no photos of finger allowed, daily 9:30–13:30 & 15:30–19:30, until 19:00 in winter). A museum in the crypt at the side entrance dedicated to the saint is worth a visit for devotees (€2, April–Oct Tue–Sun 10:00–14:00 & 16:00–19:00, Nov–March Tue–Sun 10:00–13:30 & 15:30–17:30, closed Mon, last entry 30 min before closing).

St. Teresa (1515–1582)—reforming nun, mystic, and writer—bought a house in Ávila and converted it into a convent with more stringent rules than the one she belonged to. She faced opposition in her hometown from rival nuns and those convinced her visions of heaven were the work of the devil. However, with her mentor and fellow mystic St. John of the Cross she established convents of Discalced (shoeless) Carmelites throughout Spain, and her visions and writings led her to sainthood (canonized 1622).

Yemas—These pastries, made by local nuns, are like soft-boiled egg yolks that have been cooled and sugared. They're sold all over town. The shop Las Delicias del Convento is actually a retail outlet for the cooks of the convent (€3.50 for a small box, Tue–Sat 10:30–14:00 & 17:00–20:00, Sun 10:30–18:00, closed Mon, hours and closed day vary by season, a block from TI, at Calle Reyes Católicos 12, tel. 920-220-293).

Sleeping in Ávila

(€1 = about $1.40, country code: 34)
The first hotel is antique and classy, facing the cathedral. The second is simpler and faces the wall's entrance that leads to the cathedral. Ávila is cold in fall, winter, and early spring; both hotels have heating.

$$$ Hotel Palacio de los Velada is a five-centuries-old palace with 145 elegant rooms surrounding a huge and inviting arcaded courtyard (Sb-€150, Db-€190, third person-€30 extra on weekends, lower rates Mon–Thu and for 2-night weekend stays, higher on holidays, air-con, elevator, Plaza de la Catedral 10, tel. 920-255-100, fax 920-254-900, www.veladahoteles.com, reserves .avila@veladahoteles.com).

$$ Hostal Puerta del Alcázar has 27 basic yet spacious rooms right next to the Puerta del Peso de la Harina just outside the wall (Sb-€43, Db-€55, Tb-€77, Qb-€99, includes tax and breakfast, no air-con, San Segundo 38, tel. 920-211-074, fax 920-211-075, www.puertadelalcazar.com, info@puertadelalcazar.com). Also see "Eating," next.

$$ Hotel El Rastro has 26 rooms with a modern country touch—but a stuffy staff—near Puerta del Rastro (Sb-€45, Db-€75, includes breakfast, Calle Cespedas s/n, tel. 920-352-225, fax 920-352-223, www.elrastroavila.com, info@elrastroavila.com, Pilar).

Eating in Ávila

La Bodeguita de San Segundo is a good bet for a classy light lunch. Owned by a locally famous wine connoisseur, it serves fine wine by the glass with gourmet tapas, including smoked-cod salad and wild-mushroom scrambled eggs (Thu–Tue 12:00–24:00, closed Wed, along the outside of wall near cathedral at San Segundo 19, tel. 920-257-309).

Hostal-Restaurante Puerta del Alcázar, filled with more locals than hotel guests, serves elaborate salads, fixed-price meals (for €13 and €21), and more. You can sit indoors, or even better, outdoors with cathedral views (Mon–Sat 13:30–16:00 & 21:00–23:30, Sun 13:30–16:00, San Segundo 38, tel. 920-211-074).

Café: For a pleasant break from sightseeing, pop in the courtyard of the recommended **Hotel Palacio de los Velada** for a drink (€3 coffee and hot chocolate).

Connections

The bus terminal is closed on Sundays, but you can purchase tickets when boarding the bus.

From Ávila to: Segovia (5 buses/day weekdays, 2 on weekends, 1.25 hrs), **Madrid** (1 train/hr until 21:55, 90 min, more frequent connections with Chamartín Station than Atocha; 8 buses/day, 4 on weekends, 1.5 hrs; Estación Sur de Autobuses in Madrid, tel. 914-684-200), **Salamanca** (6 trains/day, 1 hr; 4 buses/day, 2 on weekends, 1.5 hrs). Train info: tel. 902-240-202, www.renfe.es. Bus info: tel. 902-222-282, www.lasepulvedana.es.

TOLEDO

An hour south of Madrid, Toledo teems with tourists, souvenirs, and great art by day, and delicious dinners, echoes of El Greco, and medieval magic by night. Incredibly well-preserved and full of cultural wonder, the entire city has been declared a national monument.

Spain's former capital crowds 2,500 years of tangled history—Roman, Jewish, Visigothic, Moorish, and Christian—onto a high, rocky perch protected on three sides by the Tajo River. It's so well-preserved that the Spanish government has forbidden any modern exteriors. The rich mix of Jewish, Moorish, and Christian heritages makes it one of Europe's artistic highlights.

Today, Toledo thrives as a provincial capital and a busy tourist attraction. This decade has been an eventful one for Toledo. A new high-speed AVE train connection has made Toledo a quick, 30-minute ride from Madrid. While locals worried that this link would turn their town into a bedroom community for wealthy Madrileños, the already high real-estate prices minimized the impact. The city is also undergoing a major construction project: the building of a new convention center, the Palacio de Congresos Miradero (by Rafael Moneo, architect of the Los Angeles Cathedral). While the center itself remains under construction, its huge new underground parking garage and escalator into town are complete, making arrival by car much more efficient. The long-term vision is to make the old city center essentially traffic-free (except for residents' cars, public transit, and service vehicles).

Toledo remains the historic, artistic, and spiritual center of Spain. Despite tremendous tourist crowds, Toledo sits enthroned on its history, much as it was when Europe's most powerful king, Charles V, and its most famous resident artist, El Greco, called it home.

Planning Your Time

To properly see Toledo's sights—including its museums (great El Greco) and cathedral (best in Spain)—and to experience its medieval atmosphere (wonderful after dark), you'll need two nights and a day. Plan carefully for lunchtime closures and for Toledo's notorious midday heat in summer. Get an early start and stay out late... but take a rest during the unbearable summer afternoons.

Orientation to Toledo

Toledo sits atop a circular hill, with the cathedral roughly dead-center. Lassoed into a tight tangle of streets by the sharp bend of the Tajo River (called the Tejo in Portugal, where it hits the Atlantic at Lisbon), Toledo has Spain's most confusing medieval street plan. But it's a small town within its walls, with only 10,000 inhabitants (80,000 total live in greater Toledo, including its modern suburbs). The major sights are well-signposted, and most locals will politely point you in the right direction if you ask. (You are, after all, the town's bread and butter.)

The top sights stretch from the main square, Plaza de Zocodover (zoh-koh-doh-VEHR), southwest along Calle Comercio (a.k.a. Calle Ancha, "Wide Street") to the cathedral, and beyond that to Santo Tomé and more. The visitor's city lies basically along this small but central street, and most tourists never stray from this axis. Make a point to get lost. The town is small and bounded on three sides by the river. When it's time to return to someplace familiar, pull out the map or ask, "*¿Para Plaza de Zocodover?*" From the far end of town, handy bus #12 circles back to Plaza de Zocodover (see the "Bus #12 Self-Guided Tour").

Keep in mind that sights appear closer on maps than they really are, because local maps don't factor into account the slope of the hill. In Toledo, they say everything's uphill—it certainly feels that way.

Tourist Information

Toledo has three TIs. There's one at **Bisagra Gate**, in a freestanding building in the park just outside the gate (Mon–Fri 9:00–18:00, Sat 9:00–19:00, Sun 9:00–15:00, longer hours in summer, tel. 925-220-843); another on Plaza del Ayuntamiento near the **cathedral** (Mon 10:30–14:30, Tue–Sun 10:30–14:30 & 16:30–19:00, WC, tel. 925-254-030), and a third on **Plaza de Zocodover** in Casa del Mapa (daily 10:00–18:00). At any TI you can pick up the town

TOLEDO

Toledo's History

Perched strategically in the center of Iberia, for centuries Toledo was a Roman transportation hub with a thriving Jewish population. After Rome fell, the city became a Visigothic capital (A.D. 554). In 711, the Moors (Muslims) made it a regional center. In 1085, the city was reconquered by Christians, but many Moors remained in Toledo, tolerated and respected as scholars and craftsmen.

While Jews were commonly persecuted elsewhere in Europe, Toledo's Jewish community—educated, wealthy, and cosmopolitan—thrived from the city's earliest times. Jews of Spanish origin are called Sephardic Jews. The American expression "Holy Toledo" likely originated from the Sephardic Jews who eventually immigrated to America. To them, Toledo was the holiest Jewish city in Europe...Holy Toledo!

During its medieval heyday (c. 1350), Toledo was a city of the humanities, where God was known by many names. In this haven of cultural diversity, people of different faiths lived together in harmony.

Toledo remained Spain's political capital until 1561, when Philip II moved to more-spacious Madrid. Historians fail to agree why the move was made; some say that Madrid was the logical place for a capital in the geographic center of newly formed *España,* while others say that Philip wanted to separate politics from religion. (Toledo remained Spain's religious capital.) Whatever the reason, when the king moved out, Toledo was mothballed, only to be rediscovered by 19th-century Romantic travelers. They wrote of it as a mystical place...which it remains today.

map, a copy of the *Toledo Tourist and Cultural Guide,* and the monthly *Cultural Agenda,* which lists local events. The TIs share a website: www.toledo-turismo.com.

Arrival in Toledo

"Arriving" in Toledo means getting uphill to Plaza de Zocodover. As the bus and train stations are outside of town and parking can be a challenge, this involves a hike, taxi, or city bus ride.

By Train: Toledo's early-20th-century train station is Neo-Moorish and a national monument itself for its architecture and art, which celebrate the three cultures that coexisted here. From

Toledo

TO ÁVILA
VIA N-403

BULL-
RING

TO MADRID
VIA N-401

ROMAN
CIRCUS
RUINS

PICNIC
ZONE

CARDENAL TAVERA

BUS
STATION

TO CON-
SUEGRA

PUENTE
AZARQUIEL

TO
TRAIN
STN.

"EL MARTES"
FLEA
MKT.

C. DE LA CARRERA

CITY
WALLS

BISAGRA
GATE

AV. DE LA RECONQUISTA

LA VEGA

DE LA CAVA

MIRA-
DERO

PASEO
ROSA

ESCALATORS

SUBIDA LA
GRANJA

MEZQUITA

SANTA
CRUZ
MUSEUM

PUERTA
CAMBRÓN

AV.

REAL

LA MERCED

PLAZA
ZOCODOVER

HOSTEL

OLD
BRIDGE

AQUEDUCT

SAN JUAN
DE LOS
REYES

VISI-
GOTHIC
MUSEUM

POST

COMERCIO

ALFILERITOS

PUENTE
NUEVO
ALCÁNTARA

ANGEL S. TOMÉ

SINAGOGA
DE S. MARIA
LA BLANCA

MKT.

ALCÁZAR

CATHEDRAL

VICTORIO
MACHO
MUSEUM

SANTO
TOMÉ

BAJADA DEL BARCO

PASEO DE CARRETEROS

SINAGOGA
DEL TRÁNSITO

EL GRECO'S
HOUSE

POZO AMARGO

CARR. DE SAN SEB.

PATH

TAJO RIVER

TO
PARADOR

CARRETERA

CIRCUNVALACIÓN

200 YARDS

200 METERS

DCH

□ SEE DETAIL
MAPS

↗ VIEW

P PARKING

TOLEDO

the train station, it's a 20-minute hike, a €4 taxi ride, or an easy ride on bus #5, #6, or #22 to Plaza de Zocodover (leaving the station you'll see the bus stop 30 yards to the right; €1, pay on bus, confirm by asking, *"¿Para Plaza de Zocodover?"*). Consider buying a city map at the kiosk; it's better than the free one at the TI. To walk, turn right leaving the station, cross the bridge with the mighty Alcázar on your left, pass the bus station (on right), go straight through the roundabout, continue uphill to Bisagra Gate, and head into the old town to Plaza de Zocodover.

By Bus: At the bus station, buses park downstairs. Luggage lockers and a small bus-information office are upstairs opposite the cafeteria. Before leaving the station, confirm your departure time (probably 2/hr to Madrid). You can put off buying a return

Central Toledo

🔭 View
🅿 Parking
Ⓑ Bus Stop

200 YARDS
200 METERS

TO BULLRING
+ MADRID

Ⓝ

BUS STATION

BISAGRA GATE

C. DE LA CARRERA

CITY WALLS

TO TRAIN STATION

TO RING ROAD + PARADOR

🅿

MEZQUITA

CUESTA

🅿 MIRA-DERO

SANTA CRUZ MUSEUM

SUBIDA LA GRANJA

CRISTO

CADENAS SILLY

ESCALATORS

❸

❶

CERVANTES

CALLE REAL

MERCED TEND

S. ILD.

VISI-GOTHIC MUSEUM

POST

LA PLATA

COMERCIO

Ⓑ

SAN JUAN DE LOS REYES

LEO

DON

S. ROMAN

NAV. X NUNCIO

❹

ANGEL

SANTO TOMÉ

ALFONSO XII

TRINIDAD

ALCÁZAR

SINAGOGA DE SANTA MARÍA LA BLANCA

Ⓑ

S. TOMÉ

SALVADOR

MARKET

MUSEO VICTORIO MACHO

SAN JUAN DIOS

T. MORO

S. URSULA

CATHEDRAL

Ⓑ

EL GRECO'S HOUSE

PARK

S. ISABEL

❷

ℹ + CITY HALL (AYUNTAMIENTO)

RIO TAJO

SINAGOGA DEL TRÁNSITO

STREET WIDTH IS EXAGGERATED FOR CLARITY

DCH

❶ Plaza de Zocodover
❷ Mariano Zamorano Knife Workshop
❸ Mezquita del Cristo de la Luz (Mosque)
❹ Visigothic Museum
❺ Escalator to Miradero Garage

ticket until just minutes before you leave Toledo. Specify you'd like a *directo* bus, because the *ruta* trip takes longer (60 min vs. 90 min). If you miss the *directo* bus (or if it's sold out), the *ruta* option offers a peek of off-the-beaten-path Madrid suburbia; you'll arrive at the same time as taking the next *directo* bus. From the bus station, Plaza de Zocodover is a 15-minute hike, a €4 taxi ride, or a short bus ride (catch #5 or #12 downstairs; €1, pay on bus).

By Car: If you're arriving by car, you can enjoy a scenic big-picture orientation by following the *Ronda de Toledo* signs on a big circular drive around the city. You'll view the city from many angles along the Circunvalación road across the Tajo Gorge. Stop at a viewpoint or drive to Parador de Toledo, just south of town, for the view (from the balcony) that El Greco made famous in his portrait of Toledo. The best time for this trip is the magic hour before sunset, when the top viewpoints are busy with tired old folks and frisky young lovers.

The most convenient place to park is in the big new Miradero Garage at the convention center (€16/day; drive through Bisagra Gate, go uphill half a mile, look for sign on the left directing you to *Plaza del Miradero*). There is also parking farther into town at the Alcázar Garage (opposite the Alcázar—€2/hr, €18/day).

A car is useless within Toledo's city walls, where the narrow, twisting streets are no fun to navigate. Ideally, see the old town outside of car-rental time. Pick up or drop off your car on the outskirts of town; **Avis** is at the train station (Mon–Fri 9:30–13:30 & 16:30–19:30, Sat 9:30–13:30, closed Sun, handy early and late drop options, tel. 925-214-535).

By Escalator into Town: A series of escalators runs outdoors past Bisagra Gate, giving you a free ride up, up, up into town (until 22:00). You'll end up near San Ildefonso and far from Plaza de Zocodover, but it's worth it for the novelty. The other escalator, stretching from the new Miradero Garage up nearly to Plaza de Zocodover, is only helpful for people using the garage.

Helpful Hints

Local Guidebook: Consider the readable *Toledo: Its Art and Its History* (€6 big version, €5 small version, same text and photos in both, sold all over town). It explains all of the sights (which generally provide no on-site information) and gives you a photo to point at and say, "*¿Dónde está...?*"

Internet Access: You'll find **Internet Locutorio** shops with fast terminals and long hours throughout Toledo.

Tours in Toledo

▲**Tourist Train**—For a great city overview, hop on the cheesy Tren Imperial Tourist Tram. Crass as it feels, you get a 50-minute putt-putt through Toledo and around the Tajo River Gorge. It's a fine way for non-drivers to enjoy views of the city from across the Tajo Gorge (€4.50, buy ticket from convenience store at Calle de la Sillería 14, leaves Plaza de Zocodover daily on the hour from 11:00 into the evening, recorded English/Spanish commentary, tel. 925-220-300). There are no photo stops, but it goes slowly—for the best views of Toledo across the gorge, sit on the right side, not behind the driver.

For a cheap alternative to the tourist train, try the #7.1 **city bus,** which leaves Plaza de Zocodover hourly (7:50–21:50) and

Toledo at a Glance

▲▲▲Cathedral One of Europe's best, with a marvelously vast interior and great art. **Hours:** Mon–Sat 10:00–18:30, Sun 14:00–18:30. See page 117.

▲▲Santa Cruz Museum Renaissance building housing wonderful artwork, including 15 El Grecos. **Hours:** Mon–Sat 10:00–18:30, Sun 10:00–14:00. See page 123.

▲Santo Tomé Simple chapel with El Greco's masterpiece, *The Burial of the Count of Orgaz.* **Hours:** Daily 10:00–18:45, until 17:45 mid-Oct–March. See page 126.

▲Museo Victorio Macho Collection of 20th-century Toledo sculptor's works, with expansive river-gorge view. **Hours:** Mon–Sat 10:00–19:00, Sun 10:00–15:00. See page 128.

▲San Juan de los Reyes Monasterio Church/monastery intended as final resting place of Isabel and Ferdinand. **Hours:** Daily 10:00–18:45, until 17:45 in winter. See page 129.

▲Tourist Train Tacky but fun 50-minute trip through Toledo's highlights with great Tajo Gorge views. **Hours:** Daily on the hour from 11:00 until into the evening. See page 115.

Alcázar Imposing former imperial residence dominating Toledo's skyline. **Hours:** Interior closed for installation of new National Military Museum. See page 124.

Visigothic Museum Romanesque church housing the only Visigothic artifacts in town. **Hours:** Tue–Sat 10:00–14:00 & 16:00–18:30, Sun 10:00–14:00, closed Mon. See page 125.

El Greco's House Based on a lie, with no important originals by the artist who never lived there, and likely closed for renovation in 2010. See page 127.

Sinagoga del Tránsito Museum of Toledo's Jewish past. **Hours:** Tue–Sat 10:00–21:00, Sun 10:00–14:00, closed Mon. See page 127.

Sinagoga de Santa María la Blanca Synagogue that harmoniously combines Toledo's three religious influences: Jewish, Christian, and Moorish. **Hours:** Daily April–Sept 10:00–18:45, Oct–March 10:00–17:45. See page 129.

TOLEDO

offers the same classic view across the gorge.

Local Guides—Two good guides who enjoy sharing their home-town in English are **Juan José Espadas** (a.k.a. Juanjo, tel. 667-780-475, juanjo@guiadetoledo.es) and **Almudena Cencerrado** (tel. 610-765-067, almuzen@hotmail.com). For a three-hour tour, they each charge about €140 (more on weekends).

Sights in Toledo

▲▲▲Cathedral

Holy Toledo! Spain's leading Catholic city has a magnificent cathe-dral. Shoehorned into the old center (on the spot where a mosque once stood), its exterior is hard to appreciate. But the interior is so

lofty, rich, and vast that it'll have you wandering around like a Pez dispenser stuck open, whispering "Wow."

Cost and Hours: Cathe-dral tickets are sold in the shop opposite the church entrance on Calle Cardenal (€7, Mon–Sat 10:00–18:30, Sun 14:00–18:30, open earlier

for prayer only, last entry 30 min before closing, audioguide-€3, no photos, tel. 925-222-241). A modern WC is in the ticket center.

⊙ Self-Guided Tour: Wander among the pillars, thick and sturdy as a redwood forest. Sit under one and imagine a time when the lightbulbs were candles and the tourists were pilgrims—before the *No Photo* signs, when every window provided spiritual as well as physical light. The cathedral is primarily Gothic. But since it took more than 250 years to build (1226–1495)—with continu-ous embellishments after that (every archbishop wanted to leave his imprint)—it's a mix of styles, including Gothic, Renaissance, Baroque, and Neoclassical. Enjoy the elaborate wrought-iron work, lavish wood carvings, and window after colorful window of 500-year-old stained glass. Circling the interior are ornate chapels, purchased by the town's most noble families. The sacristy has a collection of paintings that would put any museum on the map.

This confusing collage of great Spanish art deserves a close look. Hire a private guide, discreetly freeload on a tour (they come by every few minutes during peak season), rent an audioguide, or follow this quick tour. Here's a framework for your visit:

High Altar: First, walk to the high altar to marvel through the iron grille at one of the most stunning altars in Spain. Real gold on wood, by Flemish, French, and local artists, it's one of the country's best pieces of Gothic art. Don't miss the finely worked

Cheap Tricks in Toledo

- Good news: Most of the city's sights charge less than €3 to enter. Or you can beat that price by going to the Sinagoga del Tránsito on Saturday afternoon or Sunday when it's free. El Greco fans can see his art for free at the Santa Cruz Museum.
- Use Toledo's public transportation for your tours. Take the bus #12 self-guided tour through town. To get to El Greco's famous viewpoint, take bus #7.1, which leaves from Plaza de Zocodover at :50 hourly until 21:50. Its circular route loops around to the vista where you can hop off, snap some photos, and wait at the same stop for the next bus to take you back.
- Shop for picnics at the city market, Mercado Municipal, and choose an atmospheric square for your meal.

gold-plated iron grille itself—considered to be the best from the 16th century in Spain. About-face to the...

Choir: Facing the high altar, the choir is famous for its fine and richly symbolic carving. It all seems to lead to the archbishop's throne in the rear center. First, look carefully at the fine alabaster relief above the throne: It shows a seventh-century Visigothic miracle, when Mary came down to give the local bishop the holy robe, legitimizing Toledo as the spiritual capital (and therefore political capital) of Spain.

Because of its primacy in Iberia, Toledo was the first city in the crosshairs of the Reconquista Christian forces. They recaptured the city in 1085 (over 400 years before they retook Granada). A local saying goes, "A carpet frays from the edges, but the carpet of Al-Andalus (Muslim Spain) frayed from the very center" (meaning Toledo). The fall of Toledo marked the beginning of the end of the Muslim domination of Iberia.

The lower wooden stalls are decorated with scenes showing the steady one-city-at-a-time finale of the Christian Reconquista, when Muslims were slowly pushed back into Africa. Set in the last decade of the Reconquista, these images celebrate the retaking of the towns around Granada: Each idealized castle has the reconquered town's name on it, culminating in the final victory at Granada in 1492 (the reliefs flank the archbishop's throne). While the castles are romanticized, the carvings of the clothing, armor, and weaponry are so detailed and accurate that historians have

Toledo's Cathedral

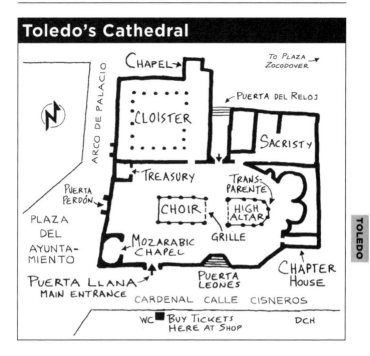

CLOISTER

CHAPEL→

To PLAZA ZOCODOVER

PUERTA DEL RELOJ

ARCO DE PALACIO

SACRISTY

←TREASURY

TRANS-PARENTE

PUERTA PERDÓN→

CHOIR

HIGH ALTAR

PLAZA DEL AYUNTA-MIENTO

MOZARABIC CHAPEL

GRILLE

CHAPTER HOUSE

PUERTA LLANA→
MAIN ENTRANCE

PUERTA LEONES

CARDENAL CALLE CISNEROS

WC ■ BUY TICKETS HERE AT SHOP

DCH

TOLEDO

studied them to learn the evolution of weaponry.

The upper stalls feature Old Testament figures—an alabaster genealogy of the church—starting with Adam and Eve and working clockwise to Joseph and "S. M. Virgo Mater" (St. Mary the Virgin Mother). Notice how the statues on the Adam and Eve side are more lifelike; they were done by Alonso Berruguete, nicknamed "the Michelangelo of Spain" for his realistic figures. All this imagery is designed to remind viewers of the legitimacy of the bishop's claims to religious power. Check out the seat backs, made of carved walnut and featuring New Testament figures—with Peter (key) and Paul (sword)—alongside the archbishop himself.

And, as is typical of choir decoration, the carvings on the misericords (the tiny seats that allowed tired worshippers to lean while they "stand") represent various sins and feature the frisky, folksy, sexy, profane art of the day. Apparently, since you sat on it, it could never be sacred anyway.

Take a moment to absorb the marvelous complexity, harmony, and cohesiveness of the art around you. Look up. There are two fine pipe organs: one early 18th-century Baroque and the other late 18th-century Neoclassical. As you leave the choir, note the serene beauty of the 13th-century Madonna and child at the front (Virgin Blanca), thought to be a gift from the French king to Spain. Its naturalism and intimacy was proto-Renaissance—

radical in its day.

The iron grille of the choir is notable for the dedication of the man who built it. Domingo de Céspedes, a Toledo ironworker, accepted the commission to build the grille for 6,000 ducats. The project, which took from 1541 to 1548, was far more costly than he anticipated. The medieval Church didn't accept cost overruns, so to finish it he sold everything he owned and went into debt. He died a poor—but honorable—man. (While that's a charming story, the artistic iron gate before the high altar is the true treasure.)

Chapter House (Sala Capitular): Face the altar, and go around it to your right to the chapter house. Under its lavish ceiling, this fresco celebrates the humanism of the Italian Renaissance. There's a Crucifixion, a *pietà*, and a Resurrection on the front wall; they face a fascinating Last Judgment, where the seven sins are actually spelled out in the gang going to hell: arrogance (the guy striking a pose), avarice (holding his bag of coins), lust (the easy woman with the lovely hair and fiery crotch), anger (shouting at lust), gluttony (the fat guy), envy, and laziness. Imagine how instructive this was in 1600.

Below the fresco, a pictorial review of 1,900 years of Toledo archbishops circles the room. The upper row of portraits dates from the 16th century. Except for the last two, these were not painted from life (the same face seems to be recycled over and over). The lower portraits were added one at a time from 1515 on and are of more historic than artistic interest. Imagine sitting down to church business surrounded by all this tradition and theology.

The current cardinal—whose portrait will some day grace the next empty panel—is the top religious official in Spain. He's as conservative as Pope Benedict XVI on issues unpopular with Spain's young: divorce, abortion, and contraception. When he speaks, it makes news all over Spain.

As you leave, notice the iron-pumping cupids carved into the pear-tree panels lining the walls.

Transparente: The *transparente*, behind the high altar, is a unique feature of the cathedral. In the 1700s, a hole was cut into the ceiling to let a sunbeam brighten Mass. Melding this big hole with the Gothic church presented a challenge, and the result was a Baroque masterpiece. Gape up at this riot of angels doing flip-flops, babies breathing thin air, bottoms of feet, and gilded sunbursts. Step back to study the altar, which looks chaotic, but is actually structured thoughtfully: The good news of salvation springs from Baby Jesus,

up past the archangels (including one in the middle who knows how to hold a big fish correctly) to the Last Supper high above, and beyond into the light-filled dome. I like it, as did (I guess) the two long-dead cardinals whose faded red hats hang from the edge of the hole. (A perk that only a cardinal enjoys is to choose a burial place in the cathedral and hang his hat over that spot until the hat rots.)

Sacristy: The cathedral's sacristy is a mini-Prado, with 18 El Grecos and masterpieces by Francisco de Goya, Titian, Peter Paul Rubens, Diego Velázquez, Caravaggio, and Giovanni Bellini. First, notice the fine perspective work on the ceiling (fresco by Lucca Giordano from Naples, c. 1690). Then walk to the end of the room for the most important painting in the collection, El Greco's *The Spoliation* (a.k.a. *Christ Being Stripped of His Garments*).

Spain's original great painter was Greek, and this is his first masterpiece after arriving in Toledo. El Greco's painting from 1579 hangs exactly where he intended it to—in the room where priests prepared themselves for Mass. It shows Jesus surrounded by a sinister mob and suffering the humiliation of being stripped in public before his execution.

The scarlet robe is about to be yanked off, and the women (lower left) avert their eyes, turning to watch a carpenter at work (lower right) who bores the holes for nailing Jesus to the cross. While the carpenter bears down, Jesus—the other carpenter— looks up to heaven. The contrast between the motley crowd gambling for his clothes and Jesus' noble face underscores the quiet dignity with which he endures this ignoble treatment. Jesus' delicate white hand stands out from the flaming red tunic with an odd gesture that's common in El Greco's paintings. Some say this was the way Christians of the day swore they were true believers, not merely Christians-in-name-only, such as former Muslims or Jews who converted to survive.

On the right is a rare religious painting by Goya, the *Betrayal of Christ,* which shows Judas preparing to kiss Jesus, thus identifying him to the Roman soldiers. Enjoy the many other El Grecos. A small-but-lifelike 17th-century carving of St. Francis by Pedro de Mena is just to the right of the Goya.

The Cloister: The cloister is likely closed through 2010. If it's open, take a peaceful detour to a funerary chapel located at the far side of the cloister from the entrance. The ceiling over the marble tomb of a bishop is a fresco by a student of Giotto (a 14th-century Italian Renaissance master).

Treasury: The *tesoro* is tiny, but radiant with riches. The highlight is the 10-foot-high, 430-pound monstrance—the tower designed to hold the Holy Communion wafer (the host) during the festival of Corpus Christi ("body of Christ") as it parades through the city. Built in 1517 by Enrique de Arfe, it's made of 5,000 individual pieces held together by 12,500 screws. There are diamonds, emeralds, rubies, and 400 pounds of gold-plated silver. The inner part (which is a century older) is 35 pounds of solid gold. Yeow. The base is a later addition from the Baroque period.

To the right of the monstrance is a beautiful red-coral cross given by the Philippines. To the right of the cross is a facsimile of a 700-year-old Bible hand-copied and beautifully illustrated by French monks; it was a gift from St. Louis, the 13th-century king of France. Imagine looking on these lavish illustrations with medieval eyes—an exquisite experience. (The precious and fragile lambskin original is preserved out of public view.) The finely painted small crucifix on the opposite side in the corner—by the great Gothic Florentine painter Fra Angelico—depicts Jesus alive on the back and dead on the front, and was a gift from Mussolini to Franco. Underneath, you'll find Franco's rather plain sword. Hmmm. Near the door, find the gift (humble amid all this splendor) from Toledo's sister city, Toledo, Ohio.

Before 10:00, the cathedral is open only for prayer (from north entrance). If you're here to worship at 9:00, you can peek into the otherwise-locked **Mozarabic Chapel** (Capilla Mozárabe). The Visigothic Mass (in Latin), the oldest surviving Christian ritual in Western Europe, starts at 9:00 (Mon–Sat). You're welcome to partake in this stirring example of peaceful coexistence of faiths. Toledo's proud Mozarabic community of 1,500 people traces its roots to Visigothic times.

In Central Toledo
Plaza de Zocodover—The main square is Toledo's center and your gateway to the old town. The word Zocodover derives from the Arabic for horse market.

Because Toledo is the state capital of Castile–La Mancha, the regional government administration building overlooks Plaza de Zocodover. Look for the three flags: one for Europe, one for Spain, and one for Castile–La Mancha. And speaking of universal symbols—find the low-key McDonald's. A source of controversy, it was finally allowed...with only one small golden arch.

The square is a big local hangout and city hub. Once the scene of Inquisition executions and bullfights, today it's a lot more peaceful. Old people arrive in the morning, and young people come in the evening. The goofy white tourist train leaves from here, as do buses #5 and #6, which lumber to the train station. Just uphill is the stop for bus #12, which travels around the old town to Santo Tomé (and works as a good self-guided tour—described at the end of the "Sights" section) and for bus #7.1, which heads out to the panoramic viewpoint made famous by El Greco.

▲▲**Santa Cruz Museum**—For years, this museum has been in a confused state of renovation—not really open, not really closed. Officials hope to create a grand city museum by incorporating this fine building with the adjacent Santa Fe monastery. During renovation, the museum's cloister and a room full of its best art are open and free. If the core of the building is filled with a temporary exhibit, you can generally wander in for a free look (Mon–Sat 10:00–18:30, Sun 10:00–14:00; from Plaza de Zocodover, go through arch to Calle Miguel de Cervantes 3).

This stately Renaissance building was an orphanage and hospital, built from money left by the humanist and diplomat Cardinal Mendoza when he died in 1495. The cardinal, confirmed as Chancellor of Castile by Queen Isabel, was so influential that he was called "the third king."

Your visit has three parts: the main building (with temporary exhibit), the fine cloister, and the museum rooms off the cloister.

The building (especially its facade, cloister arches, and stairway leading to the upper cloister) is a fine example of the Plateresque style. This ornate strain of Spanish Renaissance is named for the fancy work of silversmiths of the 16th century. During this time (c. 1500–1550), the royal court moved from Toledo to Madrid—when Madrid was a village, and Toledo was a world power. (You'll see no Plateresque work in Madrid.) Note the Renaissance-era mathematics, ideal proportions, round arches, square squares, and classic columns.

The footprint of the main building makes a Greek cross. As 1500 was a time of transition, the fine ceiling is an impressive mix of two styles: indigenous Moorish and trendier Italian Renaissance. After renovation, the wings of the building will be filled with 16th-century art, tapestries, furniture, armor, and documents.

Enjoy the peaceful cloister. In the corner stands an ignored well (now capped), bearing an Arabic inscription and grooves made by generations of Muslims pulling their buckets up by rope. The well was once in the courtyard of an 11th-century mosque that stood where the cathedral does today.

The museum section features a collection of 15 El Grecos. The highlight: the impressive *Assumption of Mary*, a spiritual poem on canvas. This altarpiece, finished one year before El Greco's death in 1614, is the culmination of his unique style, combining all of his techniques to express an otherworldly event.

Toledo's Muslim Legacy

You can see the Moorish influence in these sights:
- Mezquita del Cristo de la Luz, the last of the town's mosques
- Sinagoga del Tránsito's Mudejar plasterwork
- Sinagoga de Santa María la Blanca's mosque-like horseshoe arches and pinecone capitals
- Puerta del Sol (Gate of the Sun) and other surviving gates (with horseshoe arches) along the medieval wall
- The city's labyrinthine, medina-like streets

Study the *Assumption* (which some believe is misnamed, and actually shows the Immaculate Conception). Bound to earth, the city of Toledo sleeps, but a vision is taking place overhead. An angel in a billowing robe spreads his wings and flies up, supporting Mary, the mother of Christ. She floats up through warped space, to be serenaded by angels and wrapped in the radiant light of the Holy Spirit. Mary flickers and ripples, charged from within by her spiritual ecstasy, caught up in a vision that takes her breath away. No painter before or since has captured the supernatural world better than El Greco.

Find the lavish but faded *Astrolabe Tapestry* (c. 1480, Belgian), which shows a new view of the cosmos at the dawn of the Renaissance and the Age of Discovery: God (far left) oversees all, as Atlas (with the help of two women and a crank handle) spins the universe, containing the circular earth. The wisdom gang (far right) heralds the wonders of the coming era. Rather than a map of earth, this is a chart showing the cosmic order of things as the constellations spin around the stationary North Star (center).

Upstairs is a wonderful exhibit for tile- and ceramic-lovers. The private collection of the Carranza family has been "on loan" to the museum for the past 20 years. They began collecting tile and assorted ceramics that date from the end of the Reconquista (1492). Each piece is categorized by the Spanish region where it was made and professionally displayed. In spite of the lack of English explanations, this is the only place in Spain where you can compare regional differences in tile work and pottery.

Alcázar—This huge former imperial residence—built on the site of Roman, Visigothic, and Moorish fortresses—dominates the Toledo skyline. It's been closed for years for renovation. When it finally reopens (perhaps in 2010), it will be a boring National Military Museum.

The Alcázar became a kind of right-wing Alamo during Spain's Civil War, when Franco's Nationalists (and hundreds of hostages) were besieged for two months in 1936. Finally, after many fierce but futile Republican attacks that destroyed much of the Alcázar, Franco sent in an army that took Toledo. The place was rebuilt and glorified under Franco.

Unfortunately Spain's Civil War is still too hot a topic to address in any museum, even here at the Alcázar. While an exhibit on the major 20th-century event in Spain would be fascinating and teach valuable lessons, to this day Spain has no museum on its civil war.

Mezquita del Cristo de la Luz—Of Muslim Toledo's 10 mosques, this barren little building (dating from about 1000) is the best survivor. Looking up, you'll notice the Moorish fascina-

tion with geometry—each of the domes is a unique design. The lovely keyhole arch faces Mecca. In 1187, after the Reconquista, the mosque was changed to a church, the Christian apse (with its crude Romanesque art) was added, and the former mosque got its current name. The fine garden with its fountains is a reminder of the Quranic image of heaven (€2.30, daily 10:00–18:45, until 17:45 in winter, Cuesta de las Carmelitas Descalzas 10).

Visigothic Museum in the Church of San Roman (Museo Visigoda Iglesia de San Roman)—This 13th-century Mudejar church (with its rare, strangely modernist 13th-century Romanesque frescoes) provides an exquisite space for a small but interesting collection of Visigothic artifacts. The Visigoths were the Christian barbarian tribe who ruled Spain between the fall of Rome and the rise of the Moors. The only thing Visigothic about the actual building are the few capitals topping its columns, recycled from a seventh-century Visigothic church. While the elaborate crowns are copies (the originals are in Madrid), other glass cases show off metal and stone artifacts from the age when Toledo was the capital of the Visigoths. The items, while featuring almost no human figures, are rich in symbolism. Their portability fits that society's nomadic heritage. Archaeologists have found almost no Visigothic artifacts within Toledo's fortified hill location. They lived in humble settlements along the river—apparently needing no defense system…until the Moors swept through in 711, ending two centuries of Visigothic rule in Iberia (free, Tue–Sat 10:00–14:00 & 16:00–18:30, Sun 10:00–14:00, closed Mon). Unfortunately the museum thinks the entire world speaks Spanish: The only English explains the cost of admission.

In Southwest Toledo

These sights cluster at the southwest end of town. For efficient sightseeing, visit them in this order, then zip back home on bus #12 (listed at the end of this section).

▲**Santo Tomé**—A simple chapel on the Plaza del Conde holds El Greco's most beloved painting. *The Burial of the Count of Orgaz* couples heaven and earth in a way only The

Greek could. It feels so right to see a painting left *in situ*, where the artist placed it 400 years ago (€2.30, daily 10:00–18:45, until 17:45 mid-Oct–March, tel. 925-256-098). Go early or late to avoid long lines of tour groups.

Take this slow. Stay a while—let it perform. The year is 1323. Count Don Gonzalo Ruiz has died. You're at his burial right here in this chapel. The good count was so holy, even saints Augustine and Stephen have come down from heaven to lower his body into the grave. (The painting's subtitle is "Such is the reward for those who serve God and his saints.")

More than 250 years later, in 1586, a local priest (depicted on the far right, reading the Bible) hired El Greco to make a painting of the burial to hang over the count's tomb. The funeral is attended by Toledo's most distinguished citizens. (El Greco used local nobles as models.) The painting is divided in two by a serene line of noble faces—heaven above and earth below. Above the faces, the count's soul, symbolized by a little baby, rises up through a mystical birth canal to be reborn in heaven, where he's greeted by Jesus, Mary, and all the saints. A spiritual wind blows through as colors change and shapes stretch. This is Counter-Reformation propaganda—notice Jesus pointing to St. Peter, the symbol of the pope in Rome, who controls the keys to the pearly gates. Each face is a detailed portrait. El Greco himself (eyeballing you, seventh figure in from the left) is the only one not involved in the burial. The boy in the foreground—pointing to the two saints as if to say, "One's from the first century, the other's from the fourth…it's a miracle!"—is El Greco's son. On the handkerchief in the boy's pocket is El Greco's signature, written in Greek.

Don Gonzalo Ruiz's actual granite tombstone is at your feet. The count's two wishes upon his death were to be buried here and

El Greco
(1541–1614)

Born on Crete and trained in Venice, Doménikos Theotokópoulos (tongue-tied friends just called him "The Greek")

came to Spain to get a job decorating El Escorial. He failed there, but succeeded in Toledo, where he spent the last 37 years of his life. He mixed all three regional influences into his palette. From his Greek homeland, he absorbed the solemn, abstract style of icons. In Italy, he learned the bold use of color, elongated figures, twisting poses, and dramatic style of the later Renaissance. These elements were then fused in the fires of fanatic Spanish-Catholic devotion.

Not bound by the realism so important to his fellow artists, El Greco painted dramatic visions of striking colors and figures—bodies unnatural and lengthened as though stretched between heaven and earth. He painted souls, not faces. His work is on display at nearly every sight in Toledo. Thoroughly modern in his disregard of realism, he didn't impress the austere Philip II. But his art still seems as fresh as contemporary art does today.

TOLEDO

for his village to make an annual charity donation to feed Toledo's poor. Finally, more than two centuries later, the people of Orgaz said, "Enough!" and stopped the payments. The last of the money was spent to pay El Greco for this painting.

El Greco's House (Museo El Greco)—This small art gallery in a house built upon the spot where El Greco lived cons countless tourists with its misleading name. For better El Greco, go to the Santa Cruz Museum (described above). El Greco's House will likely be closed for renovation in 2010 (Calle Samuel Leví).

Sinagoga del Tránsito (Museo Sefardí)—Built in 1361, this is the best surviving slice of Toledo's Jewish past. Serving as Spain's national Jewish museum, it displays Jewish artifacts, including costumes, menorahs, and books. The synagogue's interior decor looks more Muslim than Jewish. After Christians reconquered the city in 1085, many Moorish workmen stayed on, beautifying the city with their unique style called Mudejar. The synagogue's intricate, geometrical carving in stucco features leaves, vines, and flowers; there are no human shapes, which are forbidden by the Torah—like the Quran—as being "graven images." In the frieze (running along the upper wall, just below the ceiling), the Arabic-looking script is actually Hebrew, quoting psalms (respected by all "people of the book"—Muslims, Jews, and Christians alike). The side-wall balcony is the traditional separate worship area for women. Scale models of the development of the Jewish quarter (on the ground floor) and video displays (upstairs) give a fuller picture of Jewish life in medieval Toledo.

This 14th-century synagogue was built at the peak of Toledo's enlightened tolerance—constructed for Jews with Christian approval by Muslim craftsmen. Nowhere else in the city does Toledo's three-culture legacy shine brighter than at this synagogue. But in 1391, just a few decades after it was built, the Church and the Spanish kings began a violent campaign to unite Spain as a Christian nation, forcing Jews and Muslims to convert or leave. In 1492, Ferdinand and Isabel exiled Spain's remaining Jews. It's estimated that, in the 15th century, a third of Spain's Jews were killed, a third survived by converting to Christianity, and a third moved elsewhere (€3, free Sat afternoon from 14:00 and all day Sun; open Tue–Sat 10:00–21:00, Sun 10:00–14:00, closed Mon; audioguide-€3, near El Greco's House on Calle de los Reyes Católicos).

▲**Museo Victorio Macho**—Overlooking the gorge and Tajo River, this small, attractive museum—once the home and workshop of the early-20th-century sculptor Victorio Macho—offers a delightful collection of his bold Art Deco–inspired work. Even if you skip the museum, enjoy the terrace view from its gate (€3, Mon–Sat 10:00–19:00, Sun 10:00–15:00, between the two *sinagogas* at Plaza de Victorio Macho 2, tel. 925-284-225).

The house itself is an oasis of calm in the city. Your visit comes in four stages: ticket room with theater, courtyard with view, crypt, and museum. The small theater in the ticket room shows a good nine-minute video (request the English-language version). Macho was Spain's first great modern sculptor. When his Republican politics made it dangerous for him to stay in Franco's Spain, he fled to Mexico and Peru, where he met his wife, Zoila. They later returned to Toledo, where they lived and worked until he died in 1966. Zoila eventually gave the house and Macho's art to the city.

Enjoy the peaceful and expansive view from the terrace. From here it's clear how the Tajo River served as a formidable moat protecting the city. Imagine trying to attack. The 14th-century bridge on the right, and the remains of a bridge on the left, connected the town with the region's *cigarrales*—mansions of wealthy families, whose orchards of figs and apricots dot the hillside even today.

The door marked *Crypta* leads to *My Brother Marcelo*—the touching tomb Macho made for his brother. Eventually he featured his entire family in his art. A dozen steps above the terrace you'll find a single room marked *Museo* filled with Macho's art.

A *pietà* is carved expressively in granite. Self-portraits show the artist's genius. Exquisite pencil on paper studies illustrate how a sculptor must understand the body (in this case, Zoila's body). Other statues show the strength of the peoples' spirit as Republicans stood up to Franco's fascist forces, and Spain endured its 20th-century bloodbath. The highlight is *La Madre* (from 1935), Macho's life-size sculpture of his mother sitting in a chair. It illustrates the sadness and simple wisdom of Spanish mothers who witnessed so much suffering. Upon a granite backdrop, her white marble hands and face speak volumes.

Sinagoga de Santa María la Blanca—This synagogue-turned-church has Moorish horseshoe arches and wall carvings. It's a vivid reminder of the religious cultures that shared (and then didn't share) this city. While it looks like a mosque, it never was one. Built as a Jewish synagogue by Muslim workers around 1200, it became a church in 1492 when Toledo's Jews were required to convert or leave—hence the mix-and-match name. After being used as horse stables by Napoleonic troops, it

was further ruined in the 19th century. Today, it's an evocative space, beautiful in its simplicity (€2.30, daily April–Sept 10:00–18:45, Oct–March 10:00–17:45, Calle de los Reyes Católicos 2).

Jewish Information Center—Casa de Jacob Librería & Judaica is a Jewish bookshop and cultural center on the street behind Santa María la Blanca. While there are books in English, most are in Spanish and Hebrew (Mon–Fri 10:00–20:00, Sun 11:00–14:00, closed Sat, Calle del Ángel 15, tel. 925-216-454, www.jewish toledo.com).

▲San Juan de los Reyes Monasterio—"St. John of the Monarchs" is a grand Franciscan monastery, impressive church, and delightful cloistered courtyard. The style is late Gothic, contemporaneous with Portugal's Manueline (c. 1500) and Flamboyant Gothic elsewhere in Europe. It was the intended burial site of the Catholic Monarchs, Isabel and Ferdinand. But after the Moors were expelled in 1492 from Granada, their royal bodies were planted there to show Spain's commitment to maintaining a Moor-free peninsula (€2.30, daily 10:00–18:45, until 17:45 in winter, San Juan de los Reyes 2, tel. 925-223-802).

The **facade** is famously festooned with 500-year-old chains. Moors used these to shackle Christians in Granada until 1492. It's said that the freed Christians brought these chains to the church, making them a symbol of their Catholic faith.

Even without the royal tombs that would have dominated the

space, the glorious **chapel** gives you a sense of Spain when it was Europe's superpower. The monastery was built to celebrate the 1476 Battle of Toro, which made Isabel the queen of Castile. Since her husband, Ferdinand, was king of Aragon, this effectively created the Spain we know today. (You could say 1476 is to Spain what 1776 is to the US.) Now united, Spain was able to quickly finish the Reconquista, ridding Iberia of its Moors within the next decade and a half.

Sitting in the chapel, you're surrounded by propaganda proclaiming Spain's greatness. The coat of arms is repeated obsessively. The eagle with the halo disk represents St. John, protector of the royal family. The yoke and lions remind people of the power of the kingdoms yoked together under Ferdinand and Isabel. The coat of arms is complex because of Iberia's many kingdoms (e.g., a lion for Lyon, and a castle for Castile). Arrows represent the 10 or so kingdoms of Iberia—weak when single, yet mighty when bound together. This notion inspired fascists such as Franco and Mussolini (who used a similar image of sticks bound together for strength). All of this is carved in actual stone, not made of stucco—rare in Toledo.

As you leave, look up over the door to see the Franciscan coat of arms—with the five wounds of the crucifixion (the stigmata—which St. Francis earned through his great faith) flanked by angels with dramatic wings.

Enjoy a walk around the **cloister**. Notice details of the fine carvings. Everything had meaning in the 15th century. In the corner (opposite the entry), just above eye level, find a monkey—an insulting symbol of Franciscans—on a toilet reading the Bible upside-down. Perhaps a

stone carver snuck in a not-too-subtle comment on Franciscan pseudo-intellectualism, with their big libraries and small brains.

Napoleon's troops are mostly to blame for the destruction of the church, a result of Napoleon's view that monastic power in Europe was a menace. While Napoleon's biggest error was to invade Russia, his second dumbest move was to alienate the Catholic faithful by destroying monasteries such as this one. This strategic mistake eroded popular support from people who might have seen Napoleon as a welcome alternative to the tyranny of kings and the Church.

▲Bus #12 Self-Guided Tour (A Sweat-Free Return Trip from Santo Tomé to Plaza de Zocodover)—When you're finished with the sights at the Santo Tomé end of town, you can hike all the way back (not fun)—or simply catch bus #12 from Plaza del Conde in front of Santo Tomé (fun!). Santo Tomé is the end of the line, so buses wait to depart from here twice hourly (at :25 and :55, until 21:55, pay driver €1), heading to Plaza de Zocodover. Closer to the synagogues and monastery, you can also catch the same bus at Plaza del Barrio Nuevo. The bus offers tired sightseers a quick, interesting 15-minute look at the town walls. Here's what you'll see on your way from Santo Tomé:

Leaving Santo Tomé, you'll first ride through Toledo's Jewish section. On the right, you'll pass El Greco's House, Sinagoga del Tránsito, and Sinagoga de Santa María la Blanca, followed by—on your left—the ornate Flamboyant Gothic facade of San Juan de los Reyes Monasterio. After squeezing through the 16th-century city gate, the bus follows along the outside of the mighty 10th-century wall. (Toledo was never conquered by force...only by siege.)

Just past the big escalator (which brings people from parking lots up into the city), the wall gets fancier, as demonstrated by the

little old Bisagra Gate. Soon after, you see the big new Bisagra Gate, the main entry into the old town. While the city walls date from the 10th century, this gate was built as an arch of triumph in the 16th century. The massive coat of arms of Emperor Charles V, with the double eagle, reminded people that he ruled a unified Habsburg/Bourbon empire, and they were entering the capital of an empire that, in the 1500s, included most of Western Europe and much of America.

The TI is just outside the big gate, at the edge of a well-maintained and shaded park—a picnic-perfect spot and one of Toledo's few green areas. After a detour to the bus station basement to pick up people coming from Madrid, you swing back around Bisagra Gate. As you climb back into the old town, notice how the modern under-construction Palacio de Congresos Miradero convention center is being incorporated into the more historic cityscape. After passing the fine Moorish (14th-century) Sun Gate, within moments you pull into the main square, Plaza de Zocodover. You can do this tour in reverse by riding bus #12 from Plaza de Zocodover to Plaza del Conde (departing at :25 and :55, same price and hours).

Shopping in Toledo

Toledo probably sells more souvenirs than any city in Spain. This is *the* place to buy medieval-looking swords, armor, maces, three-legged stools, lethal-looking letter-openers, and other nouveau antiques. It's also Spain's damascene center, where, for centuries, craftspeople have inlaid black steel with gold, silver, and copper wire. Spain's top bullfighters wouldn't have their swords made anywhere else.

Knives: At the workshop of English-speaking **Mariano Zamorano,** you can see swords and knives being made. Judging by what's left of Mariano's hand, his knives are among the sharpest (Mon–Fri 10:00–14:00 & 16:00–19:00, Sat–Sun 10:00–14:00—although you may not see work done on weekends, 10 percent discount with this book, behind Ayuntamiento/City Hall at Calle Ciudad 19, tel. 925-222-634, www.marianozamorano.com).

Damascene: Shops selling the shiny inlaid plates and decorative wares are everywhere. The damascene is a real tourist racket, but it's fun to pop into a shop and see the intricate handwork in action.

Nun-Baked Sweet Treats: Convents all over town earn a little money by selling *Dulces Artesanos.*

El Martes: Toledo's colorful outdoor market is a lively local scene on Tuesdays at Paseo de Merchan, better known to locals as "La Vega" (9:00–14:00, outside Bisagra Gate near TI).

Sleeping in Toledo

Madrid day-trippers darken the sunlit cobbles, but few stay to see Toledo's medieval moonrise. Spend the night. Hotels often have a two-tiered price system, with prices 20 percent higher on Friday and Saturday. Spring and fall are high season; November through March and July and August are less busy.

Near Plaza de Zocodover

$$–$$$ Hotel Toledo Imperial sits efficiently above Plaza de Zocodover, and rents 29 business-class rooms. Because it has no public spaces and no restaurant, it's a super value (Db-€60 Sun–Thu, Db-€100 Fri–Sat, air-con, Wi-Fi, Calle Horno de los Bizcochos 5, tel. 925-280-034, fax 925-280-205, www.hoteltoledo imperial.com, hotel@hoteltoledoimperial.com).

Near Plaza de Zocodover

DOWN TO BISAGRA GATE

CLOSED TO CARS

ALF.

NUNEN

SILLERIA

C. NUEVA

CADENAS

CALLE TOLEDO DE OHIO

CALLE

SILLERIA

COMERCIO

BARRIO REY

MC DONALDS

PLAZA DE ZOCO DOVER

ARCH

SANTA FE

CERVANTES

TO SANTA CRUZ MUSEUM

ALFERECES

TO CATHEDRAL & MOST SIGHTS

MAGDALENA CHURCH

JUAN LABRADOR

CUESTA CARLOS IV

ALCÁZAR

B BUS STOP

① Hotel Toledo Imperial
② Hotel Las Conchas
③ Hostal Centro
④ Hostal Nuevo Labrador
⑤ Pensión Castilla
⑥ Restaurante Ludeña
⑦ El Trébol & La Tabernita Tapas Bars
⑧ Supermarket Coviran
⑨ Santo Tomé Mazapán Shop
⑩ Tourist Train
⑪ Convention Center & Escalator to Miradero Garage

TOLEDO

✻ NOT TO SCALE-
PLAZA ZOCODOVER TO
MAGDALENA CHURCH IS A
3 MIN. WALK
STREET WIDTH IS
EXAGGERATED FOR CLARITY

$$ Hotel Las Conchas, a three-star hotel, gleams with marble. It's so sleek and slick it almost feels more like a hospital than a hotel. Its 35 rooms are plenty comfortable (Sb-€55; Db-€85, generally €15 less on weeknights and July–Aug; Db with terrace-€100, includes tax, 5 percent discount with this book in 2010, breakfast-€6, air-con, near the Alcázar at Juan Labrador 8, tel. 925-210-760, fax 925-224-271, www.lasconchas.com, lasconchas @ctv.es, Pablo and Yuki).

$ Hostal Centro rents 28 spacious rooms with sparse, well-worn furniture and a ramshackle feel. It's wonderfully central, with a third of its rooms overlooking the main square. Request a quiet room on the back side to minimize night noise (Sb-€35, Db-€50, Tb-€65, 10 percent discount with this book, inviting Astroturf roof terrace with sun lounge chairs, 50 yards off Plaza de Zocodover—take the first right off Calle Comercio to Calle Nueva 13, tel. 925-257-091, fax 925-257-848, www.hostalcentro.com, hostal centro@telefonica.net, warmly run by Asun and David).

$ Hostal Nuevo Labrador, with 12 simple and spacious rooms and no public spaces, is quiet, modern, and a good value (Sb-€30, Db-€50, bigger Db-€60, Tb-€65, Qb-€80, includes tax, no breakfast, air-con, elevator, Juan Labrador 10, tel. 925-222-620, fax 925-226-278, www.nuevolabrador.com, nuevolabrador @telefonica.net, César).

TOLEDO

Sleep Code

(€1 = about $1.40, country code: 34)

S = Single, **D** = Double/Twin, **T** = Triple, **Q** = Quad, **b** = bathroom, **s** = shower only. Unless otherwise noted, credit cards are accepted and rooms have air-conditioning.

      To help you easily sort through these listings, I've divided the rooms into three categories, based on the price for a standard double room with bath during high season:

   $$$ **Higher Priced**—Most rooms €90 or more.
    $$ **Moderately Priced**—Most rooms between €60-90.
     $ **Lower Priced**—Most rooms €60 or less.

$ Pensión Castilla, a dark family-run cheapie, is so humble you can imagine lashing your burro out front. It rents seven basic non-smoking rooms with ceiling fans (S-€18, Db-€30, cash only, no air-con, Calle Recoletos 6, tel. 925-256-318, Teresa doesn't speak English).

Near Bisagra Gate

$$$ Hostal del Cardenal, a 17th-century cardinal's palace built into Toledo's wall, is quiet and elegant, with a cool garden and a stuffy restaurant. This poor man's parador, at the dusty old gate of Toledo, is closest to the station, but below all the old-town action (Sb-€80, Db-€130, 20 percent cheaper mid-Dec–mid-March, 5 percent discount with this book, breakfast-€9, some free parking, *serioso* staff, enter through town wall 100 yards below Bisagra Gate, Paseo de Recaredo 24, tel. 925-224-900, fax 925-222-991, www .hostaldelcardenal.com, cardenal@hostaldelcardenal.com).

$$ Hospedería de los Reyes has 15 colorful and thoughtfully appointed rooms in a new, attractive yellow building 100 yards downhill from Bisagra Gate, outside the wall (Sb-€40–50, Db-€53–70, includes breakfast, air-con, Wi-Fi, free parking nearby on the street, Calle Perala 37, tel. 925-283-667, fax 925-283-668, www.hospederiadelosreyes.com, Alicia).

$ Hostal Puerta de Bisagra is in a sprawling old building that is fresh and modern inside. Located just across from Bisagra Gate, it's convenient for arrivals, but a long hike uphill to the action (hop any bus). Its 33 comfortable rooms are rented at some of the best prices in town (Db-€50 Sun–Thu, Db-€57 Fri–Sat and daily in peak season, breakfast-€4, air-con, Wi-Fi, Calle del Potro 5, tel. & fax 925-285-277, www.puertabisagra.com).

$ Hotel Sol, with 15 newly decorated pastel non-smoking rooms, is a good value. It's on a quiet, ugly side street between

Bisagra Gate and Plaza de Zocodover (Sb-€44, Db-€59, Tb-€72, includes tax, 10 percent discount with this book, breakfast-€4, air-con, private parking-€10/day; leave the busy main drag at Hotel Real and head 50 yards down the lane to Azacanes 8; tel. 925-213-650, fax 925-216-159, www.hotelyhostalsol.com, info@hotely hostalsol.com, José Carlos). Their 11-room **$ Hostal Sol** annex across the street is just as comfortable, smoke-free, and a bit cheaper (Sb-€36, Db-€49, Tb-€59, Qb-€72, includes tax, 10 percent discount with this book, breakfast-€4).

Deep in Toledo

$$ La Posada de Manolo rents 14 thoughtfully furnished rooms across from the downhill corner of the cathedral. Manolo Junior recently opened this fine *hostal* according to his father's vision: a comfortable place with each of its three floors themed differently—Moorish, Jewish, and Christian (Sb-€42, Db-€72, big Db-€84, includes buffet breakfast, 10 percent discount with this book when you reserve direct, air-con, Wi-Fi, no elevator, two nice view terraces, Calle Sixto Ramón Parro 8, tel. 925-282-250, fax 925-282-251, www.laposadademanolo.com, toledo@laposadade manolo.com).

$$ Hotel Eurico, fresh and new, cleverly fits 23 sleek rooms into a medieval building buried deep in the old town. The staff is friendly and the hotel offers a fine value (Sb-€55–60, Db-€70–80, Tb-€70–90, air-con, breakfast-€7, Calle Santa Isabel 3, tel. 925-284-178, fax 925-254-017, www.hoteleurico.com, reservas @hoteleurico.com).

$ Hotel Santa Isabel, in a 15th-century building two blocks from the cathedral, has 41 clean, modern, and comfortable rooms and squeaky tile hallways (Sb-€35, small old Db-€45, big new Db-€55, Tb-€70, includes tax, 5 percent discount with this book, breakfast-€5, air-con, elevator, scenic roof terrace, parking-€10/day, buried deep in old town—take a taxi instead of the bus, drivers enter from Calle Pozo Amargo, Calle Santa Isabel 24, tel. 925-253-120, fax 925-253-136, www.santa-isabel.com, santa-isabel @arrakis.es).

Outside of Town, near the Bullring

These places are on a modern street next to the bullring (Plaza de Toros, bullfights only on holidays), just beyond Bisagra Gate. In this area, parking is free on the street. The bus station is a five-minute walk away, and city buses lumber by every few minutes (all go directly to Plaza de Zocodover). There are many other similarly nondescript, comfy, and cheap places in this neighborhood.

$$$ Hotel María Cristina, a sprawling 74-room hotel, has all the comforts under a thin layer of prefab tradition (Sb-€68,

Toledo Hotels and Restaurants

1 Hostal del Cardenal

2 To Hospedería de los Reyes

3 Hostal Puerta de Bisagra

4 Hotel Sol

5 La Posada de Manolo & Madre Tierra Restaurante Vegetariano

6 Hotel Eurico & Hotel Santa Isabel

7 To Hotel María Cristina & Hostal Madrid

8 To Albergue Juvenil San Servando (Hostel)

9 To Parador de Toledo & Hotel La Almazara

10 Los Cuatro Tiempos Rest.

11 Casa Aurelio I

12 Casa Aurelio II & III (on Sinagoga) & Pizzeria Pastucci

13 Rest./Cafeteria Casón López de Toledo & La Abadia Tapas Restaurante

14 Adolfo Vinoteca

15 Restaurante-Mesón Palacios

16 Mercado Municipal (Market)

Db-€105, Tb-€142, suites-€140–170, tax not included, breakfast-€9, air-con, elevator, restaurant, parking-€12/day, Marqués de Mendigorría 1, tel. 925-213-202, fax 925-212-650, www.hotel mariacristina.com, informacion@hotelmariacristina.com).

$ Hostal Madrid has two locations on the same street with over 20 rooms and a café next door (Sb-€28, Db-€40, Tb-€54, includes tax, air-con, parking-€8/day, Marqués de Mendigorría 7 and 14, reception at #7, tel. 925-221-114, fax 925-228-113, www .hostal-madrid.net, info@hostal-madrid.net).

Hostel

The 96-bed **Albergue Juvenil San Servando** youth hostel is lavish but cheap, with small rooms for two, three, or four people (€14/ bed plus €12 obligatory *alberguista* membership, swimming pool, views, cafeteria, good management, located in 10th-century Arab castle of San Servando, 10-min walk from train station, 15-min hike from town center, over Puente Viejo outside town, tel. 925-224-554, reservations tel. 925-221-676, alberguesclm@jccm.es, no English spoken).

Outside of Town with the Grand Toledo View

$$$ Parador de Toledo, with 76 rooms, is one of Spain's best-known inns. Its guests enjoy the same Toledo view El Greco made famous from across the Tajo Gorge (Sb-€142, Db-€170, Db with view-€178, Tb-€230, Tb with view-€248, tax included, breakfast-€16, €31 fixed-price meals sans drinks in their fine restaurant overlooking Toledo, 2 windy miles from town at Cerro del Emperador, tel. 925-221-850, fax 925-225-166, www.parador.es, toledo@parador.es).

$ Hotel La Almazara was the summer residence of a 16th-century archbishop of Toledo. A hulking old place with cushy public rooms and 28 simple bedrooms (10 with views), it's truly in the country, but just 1.5 miles out of Toledo (Sb-€33, Db-€45, Db with view-€49, Tb-€62, tax not included, air-con, Carretera de Toledo Arges y Polan at kilometer 3.4, follow signs from circular Ronda de Toledo road, tel. 925-223-866, fax 925-250-562, www.hotel almazara.com, reservas@hotelalmazara.com). They serve breakfast, but not lunch or dinner (and there are no restaurants nearby).

Eating in Toledo

Dining in Traditional Elegance

A day full of El Greco and the romance of Toledo after dark puts me in the mood for game. Typical Toledo dishes include partridge *(perdiz),* venison *(venado),* wild boar *(jabalí),* roast suckling pig *(cochinillo asado),* or baby lamb *(cordero*—similarly roasted after a few weeks of mother's milk). After dinner, find a *mazapán* place (such as the Santo Tomé shops) for dessert. Restaurants generally serve lunch from 13:00 to 16:00 and dinner from 20:00 until very late (Spaniards don't start dinner until about 21:00).

Los Cuatro Tiempos Restaurante ("The Four Seasons") specializes in local game and roasts, proficiently served in a tasteful and elegant setting. They offer spacious dining with an extensive and inviting Spanish wine list. It's a good choice for a quiet, romantic dinner (€19 three-course lunches, €30 à la carte dinners, Mon–Sat 13:00–16:00 & 20:30–23:00, Sun 13:00–16:00 only, at downhill corner of cathedral, Sixto Ramón Parro 5, tel. 925-223-782).

The venerable **Casa Aurelio** has three branches, each offering traditional cooking (game, roast suckling pig, traditional soup, €40 dinners) in a classy atmosphere more memorable than the meals (generally 13:00–16:30 & 20:00–23:30, air-con). None have outdoor seating, and all are within three blocks of the cathedral: **Plaza del Ayuntamiento 4** is festive (closed Mon, tel. 925-227-716), **Sinagoga 6** is most *típico* (closed Wed, tel. 925-222-097), and **Sinagoga 1,** popular with Toledo's political class, is the newest and dressiest, with a wine cellar and more modern presentation (closed Mon, tel. 925-221-392).

Restaurante Casón López de Toledo, a fancy restaurant located upstairs in an old noble palace, specializes in Castilian food, particularly venison and partridge. As you tuck in your napkin, you'll feel like an 18th-century aristocrat (€40 fixed-price meals, €52 tasting *menu,* closed Sun, reservations smart, near Plaza de Zocodover at Calle de la Sillería 3, tel. 925-254-774).

Cafeteria Casón López de Toledo is the ground-floor version of the restaurant with the same name (previous listing). While called a "cafeteria," it's actually a quality restaurant in its own right, without the pretense you find upstairs and with a simpler and much less expensive menu (€8–10 plates, great €11 weekday lunch special; same days, address, and phone as restaurant). This is where the locals dine, enjoying the fancy restaurant's kitchen at half the price.

La Abadia Tapas Restaurante is a trendy scene, great for classy tapas and a young local crowd who want imaginative plates and quality ingredients. Their €14 "selection plate" feeds two. The front area is the bar scene. Beyond that is a labyrinth of isolated little dining rooms. I found its non-smoking room had the nicest atmosphere (daily, 20 yards downhill from Restaurante Casón López de Toledo at Plaza de San Nicolás 3, tel. 925-251-140).

Adolfo Vinoteca is the wine bar of the highly respected local chef Adolfo, who runs a famous gourmet restaurant across the street. His hope: to introduce the younger generation to the culture of fine food and wine. The bar offers up a pricey but always

top-notch list of gourmet plates (€7–15 each) and fine local wines (€2–6 per glass—don't economize here). Adolfo's son, Javier, proved to me the importance of matching each plate with the right wine. I like to sit next to the kitchen to be near the creative action. If the Starship *Enterprise* had a Spanish wine-and-tapas bar on its holodeck, this would be it. Wine is sold at shop prices with a €3–6 cork fee (daily 12:00–24:00, across from cathedral at Calle Nuncio Viejo 1, tel. 925-224-244).

Eating Simply

Restaurante-Mesón Palacios is a simple, sticky diner, serving good regional food at reasonable prices to families and tourists. Their bean soup with partridge *(judías con perdiz)* and roast suckling lamb and pig are good. They serve earlier than most restaurants—from noon and from 19:00 (€19 complete dinner with the local favorites, near Plaza de San Vicente at Alfonso X El Sabio 3, tel. 925-215-972, run by ladies' man Jesús).

Restaurante Ludeña is a classic eatery with a bar, a well-worn dining room in back, and four tables on a sunny courtyard. It's very central; locals duck in here to pretend there is no tourism in Toledo (Plaza de la Magdalena 13, tel. 925-223-384).

Madre Tierra Restaurante Vegetariano is Toledo's answer to a vegetarian's prayer. Bright, spacious, classy, air-conditioned, and tuned-in to the healthy eater's needs, its appetizing dishes are based on both international and traditional Spanish cuisine (€6–10 plates, good tea selection, great veggie pizzas, closed Mon–Tue, 20 yards below La Posada de Manolo at Bajada de le Tripería 2 near Plaza de San Justo, tel. 925-223-571).

Pizzeria Pastucci, while nondescript, is a local favorite for pizza and pasta (big €14 pizza feeds two, closed Mon, near cathedral at Calle de la Sinagoga 10).

Tapas Just Off Plaza de Zocodover: Plaza de Zocodover is busy with eateries serving edible food at affordable prices, and its people-watching scene is great. But to eat better with locals, drop by **El Trébol,** tucked peacefully away just a short block off Plaza de Zocodover. Señor Ventura seems to be the mastermind behind every new trendy bar in town, and at El Trébol he offers a menu elegant in its simplicity, a crisp interior, and an inviting outdoor terrace (daily 11:00–23:00, Calle de Santa Fe 1). The specialties are *pulgas* (fine little €2 sandwiches) and *rosea* (potato and meat with spicy sauce). **La Tabernita,** half a block away, is another good tapas bar (also a Ventura adventure) with more extensive and expensive tapas and a fun local scene. They serve a free tapa with each drink (Calle de Santa Fe 14).

Picnics: Picnics are best assembled at the city market, Mercado Municipal, on Plaza Mayor (on the Alcázar side of cathedral, with a supermarket inside open Mon–Sat 9:00–15:00 & 17:00–20:00 and stalls open mostly in the mornings until 14:00, closed Sun). This is a fun market to prowl, even if you don't need food. If you feel like munching a paper-plate-size Communion wafer, one of the stalls sells crispy bags of *obleas*—a great gift for your favorite pastor. For a picnic with people-watching, consider Plaza de Zocodover or Plaza del Ayuntamiento. The Supermarket Coviran on Plaza de la Magdalena has groceries at good prices (daily 9:30–22:00, just below Plaza de Zocodover).

And for Dessert: Mazapán

Toledo's famous almond-fruity-sweet *mazapán* is sold all over town. As you wander, keep a lookout for convents advertising their version, *Dulce Artesano*. The big *mazapán* producer is Santo Tomé (several outlets, including a handy one on Plaza de Zocodover, daily 9:00–22:00). Browse their tempting window displays. They sell *mazapán* goodies individually (two for about €1, *sin relleno*— without filling—is for purists, *de piñon* has pine nuts, *imperiales* is with almonds, others have fruit fillings). Boxes are good for gifts, but sampling is much cheaper when buying just a few pieces. Their *Toledana* is a nutty, crumbly, not-too-sweet cookie with a subtle thread of squash filling (€1.20 each).

For a sweet and romantic evening moment, pick up a few pastries and head down to the cathedral. Sit on the Plaza del Ayuntamiento's benches (or stretch out on the stone wall to the right of the TI). The fountain is on your right, Spain's best-looking City Hall is behind you, and there before you is her top cathedral, built back when Toledo was Spain's capital, shining brightly against the black night sky.

Connections

While the new AVE bullet train makes the trip to Madrid in half the time (nearly hourly, 30 min), buses depart twice as frequently. Either way, Madrid and Toledo are very easily connected.

From Toledo to Madrid: By bus (2/hr, 1–1.5 hrs, €5 one-way, *directo* is faster than *ruta*, bus drops you at Madrid's Plaza Elíptica Metro stop, Continental Auto bus company, tel. 925-223-641; you can almost always just drop in and buy a ticket minutes before departure), **by train** (AVE to Madrid's Atocha Station: nearly hourly, 30 min, €10, www.renfe.es/ave), **by car** (40 miles, 1 hr). Toledo bus info: tel. 925-215-850; train info: tel. 902-240-202.

TOLEDO

From Toledo to Other Points: To get to Granada and else-where in Spain from Toledo, assume you'll have to transfer in Madrid. See Madrid's "Connections" for information on reaching various destinations.

Route Tips for Drivers

Granada to Toledo (250 miles, 5 hours): The Granada–Toledo drive is long, hot, and boring. Start early to minimize the heat and make the best time you can. Follow signs for *Madrid/Jaén/N-323* into what some call "the Spanish Nebraska"—La Mancha (see next section). After Puerto Lapice, you'll see the Toledo exit.

Toledo to Madrid (40 miles, 1 hour): It's a speedy *autovía* north, past one last billboard to Madrid (on N-401). The highways converge into M-30, which encircles Madrid. Follow it to the left (*Nor* or *Oeste*) and take the Plaza de España exit to get back to Gran Vía. If you're airport-bound, keep heading into Madrid until you see the airplane symbol (N-II).

To drive to Atocha Station in Madrid, take the exit off M-30 for Plaza de Legazpi, then take Delicias (second on your right off the square). Parking for car return is on the north side of the train station.

TOLEDO

La Mancha

La Mancha, which is worth a visit if you're driving between Toledo and Granada, shows a side of Spain that you'll see nowhere else—vast and flat. Named for the Arabic word for "parched earth," it

makes you feel small—lost in rough seas of olive-green polka dots. Random buildings look like houses and hotels hurled off some heavenly Monopoly board. This is the setting of Miguel de Cervantes' *Don Quixote*, pub-lished in the early 17th century, after England sank the Armada and the Spanish Empire began its decline. Cervantes' star character fights doggedly for good, for justice, and against the fall of Spain and its traditional old-regime ideals. Ignoring reality, Don Quixote is a hero fighting a hopeless battle. Stark La Mancha is the perfect stage.

The epitome of *Don Quixote* country, the town of **Consuegra** (TI tel. 925-475-731) must be the La Mancha Cervantes had in mind. Drive up to the ruined 12th-century castle and joust with a windmill. It's hot and buggy here, but the powerful view overlooking the village, with its sun-bleached light-red roofs, modern concrete reality, and harsh, windy silence makes for a profound picnic (a one-hour drive south of Toledo). The castle belonged to the Knights of St. John (12th and 13th centuries) and is associated with their trip to

Jerusalem during the Crusades. Originally built from the ruins of a nearby Roman circus, it has been newly restored (€3). Sorry, the windmills are post-Cervantes, only 200 to 300 years old—but you can go inside the one that serves as the TI to see how it works (€1).

If you've seen windmills, the next castle north (above Almonacid, 8 miles from Toledo) is free and more interesting than the Consuegra castle. Follow the ruined lane past the ruined church up to the ruined castle. The jovial locals hike up with kids and kites.

TOLEDO

PRACTICALITIES

This section covers just the basics on traveling in Spain (for much more information, see *Rick Steves' Spain 2010*). You can find free advice on specific topics at www.ricksteves.com/tips.

Money

Spain uses the euro currency: 1 euro (€) = about $1.40. To convert prices in euros to dollars, add about 40 percent: €20 = about $28, €50 = about $70. (Check www.oanda.com for the latest exchange rates.)

The standard way for travelers to get euros is to withdraw money from a cash machine (called a *cajero automático*) using a debit or credit card, ideally with a Visa or MasterCard logo. Before departing, call your bank or credit-card company: Confirm that your card will work overseas, ask about international transaction fees, and alert them that you'll be making withdrawals in Europe.

To keep your valuables safe, wear a money belt. But if you do lose your credit or debit card, report the loss immediately to the respective global customer-assistance centers. Call these 24-hour US numbers collect: Visa (410/581-9994), MasterCard (636/722-7111), and American Express (623/492-8427).

Phoning

Smart travelers use the telephone to reserve or reconfirm rooms, reserve restaurants, get directions, research transportation connections, confirm tour times, phone home, and lots more.

To call Spain from the US or Canada: Dial 011-34 and then the local number. (The 011 is our international access code, and 34 is Spain's country code.)

To call Spain from a European country: Dial 00-34 followed by the local number. (The 00 is Europe's international access code.)

To call within Spain: Just dial the local number.

To call from Spain to another country: Dial 00 followed by the country code (for example, 1 for the US or Canada), then the area code and number. If calling European countries whose phone numbers begin with 0, you'll usually have to omit that 0 when you dial.

Tips on Phoning: To make calls in Spain, you can buy two different types of phone cards—international or insertable—sold locally at newsstands. Cheap international phone cards, which work with a scratch-to-reveal PIN code at any phone, allow you to call home to the US for pennies a minute, and also work for domestic calls within Spain. Insertable phone cards, which must be inserted into public pay phones, are reasonable for calls within Spain (and work for international calls as well, but not as cheaply as the international phone cards). Calling from your hotel-room phone is usually expensive, unless you use an international phone card. A mobile phone—whether an American one that works in Spain, or a European one you buy when you arrive—is handy, but can be pricey. For more on phoning, see www.ricksteves.com/phoning.

Emergency Telephone Numbers in Spain: For **police** help, dial 091. To summon an **ambulance**, call 112. For passport problems, call the **US Embassy** (in Madrid, tel. 915-872-240, after-hours emergency tel. 915-872-200) or the **Canadian Embassy** (in Madrid, tel. 914-233-250). For other concerns, get advice from your hotel.

Making Hotel Reservations

To ensure the best value, I recommend reserving rooms in advance, particularly during peak season. Email the hotelier with the following key pieces of information: number and type of rooms; number of nights; date of arrival; date of departure; and any special requests. (For a sample form, see www.ricksteves.com/reservation.) Use the European style for writing dates: day/month/year. For example, for a two-night stay in July, you could request: "1 double room for 2 nights, arrive 16/07/10, depart 18/07/10." Hoteliers typically ask for your credit-card number as a deposit.

In these times of economic uncertainty, some hotels are willing to deal to attract guests—try emailing several to ask their best rate. In general, hotel prices can soften if you do any of the following: offer to pay cash, stay at least three nights, or travel off-season. You can also try asking for a cheaper room (for example, with a bathroom down the hall), or offer to skip breakfast.

Eating

By our standards, Spaniards eat late, having lunch—their biggest meal of the day—around 13:00-16:00, and dinner starting about

21:00. At restaurants, you can dine with tourists at 20:00, or with Spaniards if you wait until later.

For a fun early dinner at a bar, build a light meal out of tapas—small appetizer-sized portions of seafood, salads, meat-filled pastries, deep-fried tasties, and so on. Many of these are displayed behind glass, and you can point to what you want. Tapas typically cost about €2 apiece, but can run up to €10 for seafood. While the smaller "tapa" size (which comes on a saucer-size plate) is handiest for maximum tasting opportunities, many bars sell only larger sizes: the *ración* (full portion, on a dinner plate) and *media-ración* (half-size portion). *Jamón* (hah-MOHN), an air-dried ham similar to prosciutto, is a Spanish staple. Other key terms include *bocadillo* (baguette sandwich), *frito* (fried), *a la plancha* (grilled), *queso* (cheese), *tortilla* (omelet), and *surtido* (assortment).

Many bars have three price tiers, which should be clearly posted: It's cheapest to eat or drink while standing at the bar *(barra)*, slightly more to sit at a table inside *(mesa* or *salón)*, and most expensive to sit outside *(terraza)*. Wherever you are, be assertive or you'll never be served. *Por favor* (please) grabs the attention of the server or bartender. If you're having tapas, don't worry about paying as you go (the bartender keeps track). When you're ready to leave, ask for the bill: *"¿La cuenta?"* To tip for a few tapas, round up to the nearest euro; for a full meal, tip about 5 to 10 percent for good service.

Transportation

By Train and Bus: For train schedules, check www.renfe.es. Since trains can sell out, it's smart to buy your tickets a day in advance at a travel agency (easiest), at the train station (can be crowded; be sure you're in the right line), or online (at www.renfe.es; when asked for your Spanish national ID number, enter your passport number). Futuristic, high-speed trains (such as AVE) can be priced differently according to their time of departure. To see if a railpass could save you money, check www.ricksteves.com/rail.

Buses pick up where the trains don't go, reaching even small villages. But because routes are operated by various competing companies, it can be tricky to pin down schedules (inquire at local bus stations or TIs).

By Plane: Consider covering long distances on a budget flight, which can be cheaper than a train or bus ride. For flights within Spain, check out www.vueling.com, www.iberia.com, or www.spanair.com; to other European cites, try www.easyjet.com and www.ryanair.com; and to compare several airlines, see www.skyscanner.net.

By Car: It's cheaper to arrange most car rentals from the US. For tips on your insurance options, see www.ricksteves.com/cdw. Bring your driver's license. For route planning, try www.viamichelin.com. Freeways come with tolls (about $4/hr), but save lots of time. A car is a worthless headache in cities—park it safely (get tips from your hotel). As break-ins are common, be sure all of your valuables are out of sight and locked in the trunk, or even better, with you or in your hotel room.

Helpful Hints

Theft Alert: Spain has particularly hardworking pickpockets. Assume beggars are pickpockets and any scuffle is simply a distraction by a team of thieves. If you stop for any commotion or show, put your hands in your pockets before someone else does. Better yet, wear a money belt.

Time: Spain uses the 24-hour clock. It's the same through 12:00 noon, then keep going: 13:00, 14:00, and so on. Spain, like most of continental Europe, is six/nine hours ahead of the East/West Coasts of the US.

Siesta and Paseo: Many Spaniards (especially in rural areas) still follow the traditional siesta schedule: From around 13:00 to 16:00, many businesses close as people go home for a big lunch with their family. Then they head back to work (and shops re-open) from about 16:00 to 20:00. (Many bigger stores stay open all day long, especially in cities.) Then, after a late dinner, whole families pour out of their apartments to enjoy the cool of the evening, stroll through the streets, and greet their neighbors—a custom called the paseo. Tourists are welcome to join this people-parade.

Sights: Major attractions can be swamped with visitors; carefully read and follow this book's crowd-beating tips (visit at quieter times of day, or—where possible—reserve ahead). At many churches, a modest dress code is encouraged and sometimes required (no bare shoulders, miniskirts, or shorts).

Holidays and Festivals: Spain celebrates many holidays, which can close sights and attract crowds (book hotel rooms ahead). For more on holidays and festivals, check Spain's website: www.spain.info. For a simple list showing major—though not all—events, see www.ricksteves.com/festivals.

Numbers and Stumblers: What Americans call the second floor of a building is the first floor in Europe. Europeans write dates as day/month/year, so Christmas is 25/12/10. Commas are decimal points and vice versa—a dollar and a half is 1,50, and there are 5.280 feet in a mile. Spain uses the metric system: A kilogram is 2.2 pounds; a liter is about a quart; and a kilometer is six-tenths of a mile.

Resources from Rick Steves

This Snapshot guide is excerpted from *Rick Steves' Spain 2010*, which is one of more than 30 titles in my series of guidebooks on European travel. I also produce a public television series, *Rick Steves' Europe,* and a public radio show, *Travel with Rick Steves.* My website, www.ricksteves.com, offers free travel information, free vodcasts and podcasts of my shows, free audio tours of major sights in Europe (for you to download onto an iPod or MP3 player), a Graffiti Wall for travelers' comments, guidebook updates, my travel blog, an online travel store, and information on European railpasses and our tours of Europe.

Additional Resources
Tourist Information: www.spain.info
Passports and Red Tape: www.travel.state.gov
Packing List: www.ricksteves.com/packlist
Cheap Flights: www.skyscanner.net
Airplane Carry-on Restrictions: www.tsa.gov/travelers
Updates for This Book: www.ricksteves.com/update.

How Was Your Trip?
If you'd like to share your tips, concerns, and discoveries after using this book, please fill out the survey at www.ricksteves.com /feedback. Thanks in advance—it helps a lot.

Spanish Survival Phrases

Spanish has a guttural sound similar to the J in Baja California. In the phonetics, the symbol for this clearing-your-throat sound is the italicized *h*.

Good day.	**Buenos días.**	**bway**-nohs **dee**-ahs
Do you speak English?	**¿Habla usted inglés?**	**ah**-blah oo-**stehd** een-**glays**
Yes. / No.	**Sí. / No.**	see / noh
I (don't) understand.	**(No) comprendo.**	(noh) kohm-**prehn**-doh
Please.	**Por favor.**	por fah-**bor**
Thank you.	**Gracias.**	**grah**-thee-ahs
I'm sorry.	**Lo siento.**	loh see-**ehn**-toh
Excuse me.	**Perdóneme.**	pehr-**doh**-nay-may
(No) problem.	**(No) problema.**	(noh) proh-**blay**-mah
Good.	**Bueno.**	**bway**-noh
Goodbye.	**Adiós.**	ah-dee-**ohs**
one / two	**uno / dos**	**oo**-noh / dohs
three / four	**tres / cuatro**	trays / **kwah**-troh
five / six	**cinco / seis**	**theen**-koh / says
seven / eight	**siete / ocho**	see-**eh**-tay / **oh**-choh
nine / ten	**nueve / diez**	**nway**-bay / dee-**ayth**
How much is it?	**¿Cuánto cuesta?**	**kwahn**-toh **kway**-stah
Write it?	**¿Me lo escribe?**	may loh ay-**skree**-bay
Is it free?	**¿Es gratis?**	ays **grah**-tees
Is it included?	**¿Está incluido?**	ay-**stah** een-kloo-**ee**-doh
Where can I buy / find...?	**¿Dónde puedo comprar / encontrar...?**	**dohn**-day **pway**-doh kohm-**prar** / ayn-kohn-**trar**
I'd like / We'd like...	**Quiero / Queremos...**	kee-**ehr**-oh / kehr-**ay**-mohs
...a room.	**...una habitación.**	**oo**-nah ah-bee-tah-thee-**ohn**
...a ticket to ___.	**...un billete para ___.**	oon bee-**yeh**-tay **pah**-rah
Is it possible?	**¿Es posible?**	ays poh-**see**-blay
Where is...?	**¿Dónde está...?**	**dohn**-day ay-**stah**
...the train station	**...la estación de trenes**	lah ay-stah-thee-**ohn** day **tray**-nays
...the bus station	**...la estación de autobuses**	lah ay-stah-thee-**ohn** day ow-toh-**boo**-says
...the tourist information office	**...la oficina de turismo**	lah oh-fee-**thee**-nah day too-**rees**-moh
Where are the toilets?	**¿Dónde están los servicios?**	**dohn**-day ay-**stahn** lohs sehr-**bee**-thee-ohs
men	**hombres, caballeros**	**ohm**-brays, kah-bah-**yay**-rohs
women	**mujeres, damas**	moo-**heh**-rays, **dah**-mahs
left / right	**izquierda / derecha**	eeth-kee-**ehr**-dah / day-**ray**-chah
straight	**derecho**	day-**ray**-choh
When do you open / close?	**¿A qué hora abren / cierran?**	ah kay **oh**-rah **ah**-brehn / thee-**ay**-rahn
At what time?	**¿A qué hora?**	ah kay **oh**-rah
Just a moment.	**Un momento.**	oon moh-**mehn**-toh
now / soon / later	**ahora / pronto / más tarde**	ah-**oh**-rah / **prohn**-toh / mahs **tar**-day
today / tomorrow	**hoy / mañana**	oy / mahn-**yah**-nah

In the Restaurant

I'd like / We'd like...	**Quiero / Queremos...**	kee-**ehr**-oh / kehr-**ay**-mohs
...to reserve...	**...reservar...**	ray-sehr-**bar**
...a table for one / two.	**...una mesa para uno / dos.**	oo-nah **may**-sah **pah**-rah oo-noh / dohs
Non-smoking.	**No fumadores.**	noh foo-mah-**doh**-rays
Is this table free?	**¿Está esta mesa libre?**	ay-**stah** ay-stah **may**-sah lee-bray
The menu (in English), please.	**La carta (en inglés), por favor.**	lah **kar**-tah (ayn een-**glays**) por fah-**bor**
service (not) included	**servicio (no) incluido**	sehr-**bee**-thee-oh (noh) een-kloo-**ee**-doh
cover charge	**precio de entrada**	**pray**-thee-oh day ayn-**trah**-dah
to go	**para llevar**	**pah**-rah yay-**bar**
with / without	**con / sin**	kohn / seen
and / or	**y / o**	ee / oh
menu (of the day)	**menú (del día)**	may-**noo** (dayl **dee**-ah)
specialty of the house	**especialidad de la casa**	ay-spay-thee-ah-lee-**dahd** day lah **kah**-sah
tourist menu	**menú de turista**	meh-**noo** day too-**ree**-stah
combination plate	**plato combinado**	**plah**-toh kohm-bee-**nah**-doh
appetizers	**tapas**	**tah**-pahs
bread	**pan**	pahn
cheese	**queso**	**kay**-soh
sandwich	**bocadillo**	boh-kah-**dee**-yoh
soup	**sopa**	**soh**-pah
salad	**ensalada**	ayn-sah-**lah**-dah
meat	**carne**	**kar**-nay
poultry	**aves**	**ah**-bays
fish	**pescado**	pay-**skah**-doh
seafood	**marisco**	mah-**ree**-skoh
fruit	**fruta**	**froo**-tah
vegetables	**verduras**	behr-**doo**-rahs
dessert	**postres**	**poh**-strays
tap water	**agua del grifo**	**ah**-gwah dayl **gree**-foh
mineral water	**agua mineral**	**ah**-gwah mee-nay-**rahl**
milk	**leche**	**lay**-chay
(orange) juice	**zumo (de naranja)**	**thoo**-moh (day nah-**rahn**-hah)
coffee	**café**	kah-**feh**
tea	**té**	tay
wine	**vino**	**bee**-noh
red / white	**tinto / blanco**	**teen**-toh / **blahn**-koh
glass / bottle	**vaso / botella**	**bah**-soh / boh-**tay**-yah
beer	**cerveza**	thehr-**bay**-thah
Cheers!	**¡Salud!**	sah-**lood**
More. / Another.	**Más. / Otro.**	mahs / **oh**-troh
The same.	**El mismo.**	ehl **mees**-moh
The bill, please.	**La cuenta, por favor.**	lah **kwayn**-tah por fah-**bor**
tip	**propina**	proh-**pee**-nah
Delicious!	**¡Delicioso!**	day-lee-thee-**oh**-soh

For hundreds more pages of survival phrases for your trip to Spain, check out *Rick Steves' Spanish Phrase Book*.

Rick Steves ®
EUROPEAN TOURS

ADRIATIC • ATHENS & THE HEART OF GREECE • BARCELONA & MADRID • BELGIUM & HOLLAND • BERLIN, VIENNA & PRAGUE BEST OF EUROPE • BEST OF ITALY • BEST OF TURKEY • EASTERN EUROPE • ENGLAND FAMILY EUROPE • GERMANY, AUSTRIA & SWITZERLAND • HEART OF ITALY IRELAND • ISTANBUL • LONDON • PARIS PARIS & HEART OF FRANCE • PARIS & SOUTH OF FRANCE • PORTUGAL • PRAGUE ROME • SAN SEBASTIAN & BASQUE COUNTRY SCANDINAVIA • SCOTLAND • SICILY SOUTH ITALY • SPAIN & MOROCCO ST. PETERSBURG, TALINN & HELSINKI VENICE, FLORENCE & ROME • VILLAGE FRANCE • VILLAGE ITALY • VILLAGE TURKEY

VISIT **TOURS.RICKSTEVES.COM**

Great guides, small groups, no grumps

▶ Plan Your Trip

Browse thousands of articles and a wealth of money-saving tips for planning your dream trip. You'll find up-to-date information on Europe's best destinations, packing smart, getting around, finding rooms, staying healthy, avoiding scams and more.

▶ Eurail Passes

Find out, step-by-step, if a rail pass makes sense for your trip—and how to avoid buying more than you need. Get a bunch of free extras!

▶ Graffiti Wall & Travelers' Helpline

Learn, ask, share—our online community of savvy travelers is a great resource for first-time travelers to Europe, as well as seasoned pros.

Rick Steves' Europe Through the Back Door, Inc.

turn your travel dreams into affordable reality

▶ Free Audio Tours & Travel Newsletter

Get your nose out of this guide-book and focus on what you'll be seeing with Rick's free audio tours of the greatest sights in Paris, Rome, Florence and Venice.

Subscribe to our free *Travel News* e-newsletter, and get monthly articles from Rick on what's happening in Europe.

▶ Great Gear from Rick's Travel Store

Pack light and right—on a budget—with Rick's custom-designed carry-on bags, roll-aboards, day packs, travel accessories, guidebooks, journals, maps and DVDs of his TV shows.

130 Fourth Avenue North, PO Box 2009 • Edmonds, WA 98020 USA
Phone: (425) 771-8303 • Fax: (425) 771-0833 • www.ricksteves.com

Rick Steves

www.rickssteves.com

TRAVEL SKILLS
Europe Through the Back Door

EUROPE GUIDES
Best of Europe
Eastern Europe
Europe 101
European Christmas
Postcards from Europe

COUNTRY GUIDES
Croatia & Slovenia
England
France
Germany
Great Britain
Ireland
Italy
Portugal
Scandinavia
Spain
Switzerland

CITY & REGIONAL GUIDES
Amsterdam, Bruges & Brussels
Athens & The Peloponnese
Budapest
Florence & Tuscany
Istanbul
London
Paris
Prague & The Czech Republic
Provence & The French Riviera
Rome
Venice
Vienna, Salzburg & Tirol

PHRASE BOOKS & DICTIONARIES
French
French, Italian & German
German
Italian
Portuguese
Spanish

RICK STEVES' EUROPE DVDs
Austria & The Alps
Eastern Europe
England
Europe
France & Benelux
Germany & Scandinavia
Greece, Turkey, Israel & Egypt
Ireland & Scotland
Italy's Cities
Italy's Countryside
Rick Steves' European Christmas
Spain & Portugal
Travel Skills & "The Making Of"

PLANNING MAPS
Britain, Ireland & London
Europe
France & Paris
Germany, Austria & Switzerland
Ireland
Italy
Spain & Portugal

JOURNALS
Rick Steves' Pocket Travel Journal
Rick Steves' Travel Journal

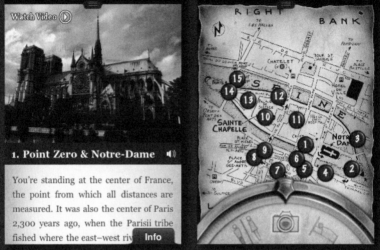

With these apps you can:

► Spin the compass icon to switch views between sights, hotels, and restaurant selections—and get details on cost, hours, address, and phone number.

► Tap any point on the screen to read Rick's detailed information, including history and suggested viewpoints.

► Get a deeper view into Rick's tours with audio and video segments.

Go to iTunes to download the following apps:

Rick Steves' Louvre Tour

Rick Steves' Historic Paris Walk

Rick Steves' Orsay Museum Tour

Rick Steves' Versailles

Rick Steves' Ancient Rome Tour

Rick Steves' St. Peter's Basilica Tour

Once downloaded, these apps are completely self-contained on your iPhone or iPod Touch, so you will not incur pricey roaming charges during use overseas.

Rick Steves books and DVDs are available at bookstores and through online booksellers.

Rick Steves guidebooks are published by Avalon Travel, a member of the Perseus Books Group.

Rick Steves apps are produced by Übermind, a boutique Seattle-based software consultancy firm.

Avalon Travel
a member of the Perseus Books Group
1700 Fourth Street
Berkeley, CA 94710

Text © 2009 by Rick Steves
Maps © 2009 Europe Through the Back Door. All rights reserved.
Printed in the US by Worzalla. First printing September 2009.
Portions of this book originally appeared in Rick Steves' Spain 2010.

For the latest on Rick Steves' lectures, guidebooks, tours, public television series, and public radio show, contact Europe Through the Back Door, Box 2009, Edmonds, WA 98020, tel. 425/771-8303, fax 425/771-0833, www.ricksteves.com, rick@ricksteves.com.

ISBN (13) 978-1-59880-490-4

Europe Through the Back Door Managing Editor: Risa Laib
ETBD Editors: Cameron Hewitt, Tom Griffin, Gretchen Strauch, Jennifer Madison Davis, Cathy Lu, Cathy McDonald, Sarah McCormic
Research Assistance: Amanda Buttinger
Avalon Travel Senior Editor and Series Manager: Madhu Prasher
Avalon Travel Project Editor: Kelly Lydick
Copy Editor: Amy Scott
Proofreader: Jean Butterfield
Production and Typesetting: McGuire Barber Design
Cover Design: Kimberly Glyder Design
Graphic Content Director: Laura VanDeventer
Maps and Graphics: David C. Hoerlein, Lauren Mills, Laura VanDeventer, Barb Geisler, Mike Morgenfeld
Cover Photo: Plaza Mayor © Vinicius Tupinamba/dreamstime.com
Photography: David C. Hoerlein, Rick Steves, Cameron Hewitt, Robert Wright, Steve Smith, Dominic Bonuccelli, and Cathy McDonald

Although the author and publisher have made every effort to provide accurate, up-to-date information, they accept no responsibility for loss, injury, soggy paella, or inconvenience sustained by any person using this book.

ABOUT THE AUTHOR

RICK STEVES

Rick Steves is on a mission: to help make European travel accessible and meaningful for Americans. Rick has spent four months every year since 1973 exploring Europe. He's researched and written more than 30 travel guidebooks, writes and hosts the public television series *Rick Steves' Europe*, and also produces and hosts the weekly public radio show *Travel with Rick Steves*. With the help of his hardworking staff of 70 at Europe Through the Back Door, Rick organizes tours of Europe and offers an information-packed website (www. ricksteves.com). Rick, his wife (and favorite travel partner) Anne, and their two teenage children, Andy and Jackie, call Edmonds, just north of Seattle, home.